NO EASY
ANSWERS

NO EASY ANSWERS

William Lane Craig

MOODY PRESS
CHICAGO

ISBN: 0-8024-2283-7

3 4 5 6 Printing/BC/Year 94 93 92 91

In Memoriam

Edward John Carnell
1919-1967

who would brook
no easy answers

Contents

Preface

This book grew out of a series of sermons preached at Fox Valley Evangelical Free Church in Algonquin, Illinois, on "Unpopular Themes," that is to say, subjects rarely discussed from the pulpit because of the hard questions they make us face. Ella Lindvall of Moody Press was among the parishioners and encouraged me to expand the series into a book that could be of practical help to Christian laymen.

This is my first attempt at a devotional-style book. I hope the reader will find it characterized by honesty and clarity and that it will aid him in dealing with issues that he confronts in his daily Christian walk. I anticipate that it will be particularly helpful to students and to their parents or teachers, who often are called upon to answer their searching questions.

As always, I am indebted to my wife, Jan, for her typing of the manuscript, as well as for her suggestions concerning the book's content.

WILLIAM LANE CRAIG

Introduction:

In Intellectual Neutral

A couple of years ago, two books appeared that sent shock waves through the American educational community. The first of these, *Cultural Literacy: What Every American Needs to Know*, by E. D. Hirsch, documented the fact that large numbers of American college students do not have the basic background knowledge to understand the front page of a newspaper or to act responsibly as a citizen. For example, a quarter of the students in a recent survey thought Franklin D. Roosevelt was president during the Vietnam War. Two-thirds did not know when the Civil War occurred. One-third thought Columbus discovered the New World sometime after 1750. In a recent survey at California State University at Fullerton, over half the students could not identify Chaucer or Dante. Ninety percent did not know who Alexander Hamilton was, despite the fact that his picture is on every ten dollar bill.

These statistics would be funny if they weren't so alarming. What has happened to our schools that they should be producing such dreadfully ignorant people? Enter Alan Bloom, an eminent educator at the University of Chicago and the author of the second book I referred to above, *The Closing of the American Mind*. Bloom's thesis, which the *Washington Times* has characterized as both "frightening" and "convincing," is that behind the current educational malaise lies the universal conviction of students that all truth is relative and, therefore, that truth is not worth pursuing. Bloom writes,

> There is one thing a professor can be absolutely certain of: almost every student entering the university believes, or says he believes, that truth is relative. If this belief is put to the test, one can count on the students' reaction: they will be uncomprehending. That anyone should regard the proposition as not self-evident astonishes them, as though he were calling into question $2 + 2 = 4$. These are things you don't think about. . . . That it is a moral issue for students is revealed by the character of their response when challenged—a combination of disbelief and indignation: "Are you an absolutist?," the only alternative they know, uttered in the same tone as . . . "Do you really believe in witches?" This latter leads into the indignation, for someone who believes in witches might well be a witch-hunter or a Salem judge. The danger they have been taught to fear from absolutism is not error but intolerance. Relativism is necessary to openness; and this is the virtue, the only virtue, which all primary education for more than fifty years has dedicated itself to inculcating. Openness—and the relativism that makes it the only plausible stance in the face of various claims to truth and various ways of life and kinds of human beings—is the great insight of our times. . . . The study of history and of culture teaches that all the world was mad in the past; men always thought they were right, and that led to wars, persecutions, slavery, xenophobia, racism, and chauvinism. The point is not to correct the mistakes and really be right; rather it is not to think you are right at all.[1]

Since there is no absolute truth, since everything is relative, the purpose of an education is not to learn truth or master facts—rather it is merely to learn a skill so that one can go out and acquire wealth, power, and fame. Truth has become irrelevant.

Now, of course, this sort of relativistic attitude is antithetical to the Christian world view. For as Christians we

1. Alan Bloom, *The Closing of the American Mind* (New York: Simon & Schuster, 1987), pp. 25-26.

believe that all truth is God's truth, that God has revealed to us the truth, both in His Word and in Him who said, "I am the Truth." The Christian, therefore, can never look on the truth with apathy or disdain. Rather, he cherishes and treasures the truth as a reflection of God Himself. Nor does his commitment to truth make the Christian intolerant, as Bloom's students erroneously inferred; on the contrary, the very concept of tolerance entails that one disagree with that which one tolerates. The Christian is committed to both truth and tolerance, for he believes in Him who said not only, "I am the Truth," but also, "Love your enemies."

Now as a teacher at a Christian liberal arts college, I began to wonder: how much have Christian students been infected with the attitude that Bloom describes? How would my own students fare on one of E. D. Hirsch's tests? *Well, how would they?* I thought. *Why not give them such a quiz?* So I did.

I drew up a brief, general knowledge quiz about famous people, places, and things and administered it to two classes of about fifty sophomores. What I found was that although they did better than the general student population, still there were sizable portions of the group who could not identify—even with a phrase—some important names and events. For example, 18 percent did not know who Mikhail Gorbachev is. Forty-nine percent could not identify Leo Tolstoi, the author of perhaps the world's greatest novel, *War and Peace.* To my surprise, 16 percent did not know who Winston Churchill was. One student thought he was one of the founding Fathers of our nation! Another identified him as a great revival preacher of a few hundred years ago! Twenty-two percent did not know what Afghanistan is, and 22 percent could not identify Nicaragua. Twenty percent did not know where the Amazon River is. Imagine!

They fared even worse with things and events. I was amazed that a whopping 67 percent could not identify the Battle of the Bulge. Several identified it as a dieter's problem. Twenty-four percent did not know what the Special

Theory of Relativity is (mind you, just to identify it—even as, say, "a theory of Einstein"—not to explain it). Forty-five percent couldn't identify Custer's Last Stand—it was variously classed as a battle in the Revolutionary War or as a battle in the Civil War. And I wasn't really surprised that 73 percent did not know what the expression *Manifest Destiny* referred to.

So it became clear to me that Christian students have not been able to rise above the dark undertow in our educational system at the primary and secondary levels. That level of ignorance presents a real crisis for Christian colleges and seminaries.

But an even more terrible fear began to dawn on me as I contemplated these statistics. If Christian students are this ignorant of the general facts of history and geography, then the chances are that they, and Christians in general, are equally or even more ignorant of the facts of our own Christian heritage and doctrine. Our culture in general has sunk to the level of biblical and theological illiteracy. A great many, if not most, people cannot even name the four gospels—in a recent survey one person identified them as Matthew, Mark, and Luther! The suspicion arose in my mind that the evangelical church is probably also caught somewhere higher up in this same downward spiral.

But if we do not preserve the truth of our own Christian heritage and doctrine, who will learn it for us? Non-Christians? That hardly seems likely. If the church does not treasure her own Christian truth, then it will be lost to her forever. So how, I wondered, would Christians fare on a quiz over general facts of Christian history and doctrine?

Well, how would they? I now invite the reader to get out a pencil and paper and take the following quiz himself. (Go on, it'll only take a minute!) The following are items I think any mature Christian in our society ought to be able to identify. Simply provide some identifying phrase that indicates that you know what the item is. For example, for "John Wesley" you might write: "the founder of Methodism" or "an eighteenth-century English revivalist."

Quiz

1. Martin Luther
2. Two natures united in one person
3. Augustine
4. Council of Nicea
5. Pantheism
6. Thomas Aquinas
7. Trinity
8. Reformation
9. Substitutionary atonement
10. Enlightenment

How did you do? If you are typical of the audiences to whom I've given this quiz, probably not too well. If that is the case, you might be tempted to react to this quiz defensively: "Who needs to know all this stuff anyway? This isn't important. All that really counts is my walk with Christ and my sharing Him with others. Who cares about all this other trivia?"

I hope that is not your reaction, for that will close you off to self-improvement, and the exercise will have been of no profit to you. You will have learned nothing from it.

But there's a second, more positive reaction. You may see, perhaps for the first time, that there is a need for you to become intellectually engaged as a Christian, and you may resolve to do something about it. That will be a momentous decision. You will be taking a step millions of Christians in the United States need to take. No one has issued a more forceful challenge to Christians to become intellectually engaged than did Charles Malik, former Lebanese ambassador to the United States, in the address he gave in 1980 at the dedication of the Billy Graham Center in Wheaton, Illinois. Malik emphasized that as Christians we face two tasks in our evangelism: saving the soul and saving the mind, that is to say, not only converting people spiritually, but converting them intellectually as well. And the church is lagging dangerously behind with regard to this second task. Mark his words well:

I must be frank with you: the greatest danger confronting American evangelical Christianity is the danger of anti-intellectualism. The mind in its greatest and deepest reaches is not cared for enough. But intellectual nurture cannot take place apart from profound immersion for a period of years in the history of thought and the spirit. People who are in a hurry to get out of the university and start earning money or serving the church or preaching the gospel have no idea of the infinite value of spending years of leisure conversing with the greatest minds and souls of the past, ripening and sharpening and enlarging their powers of thinking. The result is that the arena of creative thinking is vacated and abdicated to the enemy. Who among evangelicals can stand up to the great secular or naturalistic or atheistic scholars on their own terms of scholarship? Who among evangelical scholars is quoted as a normative source by the greatest secular authorities on history or philosophy or psychology or sociology or politics? Does the evangelical mode of thinking have the slightest chance of becoming the dominant mode in the great universities of Europe and America that stamp our entire civilization with their spirit and ideas?[2]

Malik went on to say:

It will take a different spirit altogether to overcome this great danger of anti-intellectualism. For example, I say this different spirit, so far as philosophy alone—the most important domain for thought and intellect—is concerned, must see the tremendous value of spending an entire year doing nothing but poring intensely over the *Republic* or the *Sophist* of Plato, or two years over the *Metaphysics* or the *Ethics* of Aristotle, or three years over the *City of God* of Augustine. But if a start is made now on a crash program in this and other domains, it will take at least a century to catch up with the Harvards and Tübingens and the Sorbonnes—and by then where will these universities be? For the sake of greater effectiveness in witnessing to Jesus Christ Himself, as well as for their own sakes, evangelicals cannot afford to

2. Charles Malik, "The Other Side of Evangelism," *Christianity Today*, November 7, 1980, 40.

keep on living on the periphery of responsible intellectual existence.[3]

Those are powerful words. Evangelicals really have been living on the periphery of responsible intellectual existence. The average Christian does not realize that there is an intellectual war going on in the universities and in the professional journals and scholarly societies. Christianity is being attacked from all sides as irrational, and millions of students, our future generation of leaders, have absorbed that viewpoint.

This is a war we cannot afford to lose. J. Gresham Machen warned on the eve of the Fundamentalist Controversy, that if the evangelical community lost the intellectual battle in his generation, then evangelism would be immeasurably more difficult in the next generation:

> False ideas are the greatest obstacles to the reception of the gospel. We may preach with all the fervor of a reformer and yet succeed only in winning a straggler here and there, if we permit the whole collective thought of the nation or of the world to be controlled by ideas which, by the resistless force of logic, prevent Christianity from being regarded as anything more than a harmless delusion. Under such circumstances, what God desires us to do is to destroy the obstacle at its root.[4]

Machen's warning went unheeded, and biblical Christianity retreated into the intellectual closets of Fundamentalism, from which it has only recently begun to re-emerge. The war is not yet lost, and it is one which must not be lost: souls of men hang in the balance.

What are evangelicals doing to win this war? Until recently, very little indeed. Most prominent evangelical scholars tend to be big fish in a small pond. Their influence

3. Ibid.
4. J. Gresham Machen, "Christianity and Culture," *Princeton Theological Review* 11 (1913):7.

extends little beyond the evangelical subculture. They tend to publish exclusively with evangelical presses, and therefore their books are likely to be unread by nonevangelical scholars; and instead of participating in the standard professional societies, they are active instead in the evangelical professional societies. As a result, they effectively put their light under a bushel and have little leavening effect for the gospel in their professional fields. In turn, the intellectual drift of the culture at large continues to degenerate into secularism.

We desperately need Christian scholars who can, as Malik said, compete with non-Christian thinkers in their fields of expertise on their own terms of scholarship. It can be done. There is, for example, a revolution going on right now in American philosophy. Christian philosophers have been coming out of the evangelical closet and defending the truth of the Christian world view with philosophically sophisticated arguments in the finest secular journals and societies. The face of American philosophy has been changed as a result.

Thirty years ago philosophers widely regarded talk about God as literally meaningless, as mere jibberish, but today no informed philosopher could take such a viewpoint. In fact, many of America's finest philosophers today are outspoken Christians. According to the respected philosopher Roderick Chisholm, himself no evangelical, the reason atheism was so influential a generation ago was because the brightest philosophers were atheists. But today, he says, "the brightest people include theists, using a kind of tough-minded intellectualism" that had been lacking on their side of the debate.[5] This sort of scholarship represents the best hope for the revolution that Malik and Machen envisioned, and its true impact for the cause of Christ will only be felt in the next generation.

So it can be done! What is sad, however, is how little support the evangelical church gives its thinkers, whom she

5. Roderick Chisholm, "Modernizing the Case for God," *Time,* April 7, 1980, pp. 65-66.

so desperately needs. It is ironic that it is only after an evangelical student has earned his doctorate that the Christian community pays any attention to him. Once he has his Ph.D. he receives all sorts of invitations to fill speaking engagements, and people ask him to autograph his books for them—but when he was struggling to earn his doctorate he was virtually ignored by the evangelical community or even derided as a "perpetual student." Many of the young men and women who will be needed if the evangelical community is to regain intellectual respectability live on shoestring budgets or go deeply into debt during their years of academic training, alone and forgotten, working under tremendous stress and anxiety and facing an uncertain future.

I consider it a tremendous privilege to set aside a portion of our family's giving to the Lord's work for certain of these young scholars whom we know personally and who will be our Christian leaders of tomorrow. I strongly urge churches to allocate a portion of their yearly budgets for the support of graduate school students from their congregations, especially those attending seminary or completing doctorates. Candidates for such support should be interviewed just like missionary candidates and assessed in terms of their personal spiritual lives, academic abilities, and promise for the future—for the work that they do is just as much a part of the overall evangelistic enterprise as is the work of the missionary. The church cannot in good conscience go on ignoring such persons.

What is shocking, too, is how the anti-intellectualism of which Malik spoke has become ensconced even in our evangelical institutions of higher learning. Serious scholarship is often depreciated and impeded, as professors are overburdened with large teaching loads, time-consuming committee assignments, and other administrative chores.

Scholarship seems to be almost last on the list of priorities. Moreover, my own experience as a seminary professor made clear to me that though there was a strong commitment to producing pastors, there was in the administration very little burden for producing first-rate scholars. Evangelical thought and theology will never assume a leading position in the world so long as this sort of Bible-school mentality reigns.

My personal impressions were recently confirmed by a sobering report entitled "The State of Scholarship at Evangelical Institutions," a study carried out by University of Notre Dame professor Nathan Hatch and funded by the Pew Charitable Trusts. Hatch discovered that whereas evangelical colleges and seminaries give lip service to scholarship, what they are usually talking about is a broad concept that equates "scholarship" with *any* form of publishing, even on the most popular level. But scholarship narrowly defined as "intensive, time-consuming study and writing on specialized subjects directed at others in one's field" is seriously lacking.

These two concepts of "scholarship" lead to conflicting data: thus the dean of one school claims that 90 percent of the faculty are "actively engaged" in scholarly work, whereas a faculty member *at the same institution* estimates that only 10-15 percent are engaged in scholarship, commenting that the other "75-80 percent *think* they are writing for scholarly audiences. . . . But they don't understand what it is."

Hatch's survey of fifty-eight Christian colleges and seminaries led him to conclude, "For all their dynamism and success in popular communication, evangelicals as a group are failing to sustain a serious intellectual life, conceding intellectual inquiry and discourse to those with secular presuppositions."

This conclusion would be bad enough; but Hatch's survey revealed two more deeply disturbing facts. First, *Christian college and seminary administrators generally do not appreciate serious scholarship and sometimes even impede it.* "The survey shows that college and seminary leadership generally do not make scholarship a priority," writes Hatch. Serious scholarship is "more likely to be seen as superfluous or even opposed to the institution's primary goal," which is either teaching (colleges) or else training pastors (seminaries). With regard to evangelical seminaries, scholarship is valued only "when it contributes to the central goal of training pastors, but not when it takes time away from the classroom." Second, *serious scholarship is seen as irrelevant to one's spiritual life and the life of the church.* Hatch states, "Administrators at evangelical institutions may value scholarship because it enhances teaching or because it enhances the reputation of their schools, but generally scholarship is not regarded as important to the Church's mission or to the spiritual growth of the individual."

He concludes, "Despite the rhetorical emphasis on integration of faith and learning which is commonplace at evangelical institutions, responses to this survey demonstrate that the evangelical academic world as a whole does not connect scholarship with Christian spirituality and the long-term vitality of the Church."

How tragically short-sighted such attitudes are!

Machen observed that in his day "many would have the seminaries combat error by attacking it as it is taught by its popular exponents" instead of confusing students "with a lot of German names unknown outside the walls of the university." But to the contrary, Machen insisted, it is essential that Christian scholars be alert to the power of an idea before it has reached popular formulation. Scholarly procedure, he said,

> is based simply upon a profound belief in the pervasiveness of ideas. What is today a matter of academic speculation begins tomorrow to move armies and pull down empires. In that second stage, it has gone too far to be combatted; the time to stop it was when it was still a matter of impassionate debate. So as Christians we should try to mold the thought of the world in such a way as to make the acceptance of Christianity something more than a logical absurdity.[6]

Like Malik, Machen also believed that "the chief obstacle to the Christian religion today lies in the sphere of the intellect"[7] and that objections to Christianity must be attacked

6. Machen, p. 7.
7. Ibid., p. 10.

in that sphere. "The Church is perishing to-day through the lack of thinking, not through an excess of it."[8]

What is ironic about the mentality which says that our seminaries should produce pastors, not scholars, is that it is precisely our future pastors, not just our future scholars, who have need of this scholarly training. Machen's article was originally given as a speech entitled "The Scientific Preparation of the Minister." A model for us here ought to be a man like John Wesley, a Spirit-filled revivalist and at the same time an Oxford-educated scholar.

In 1756 Wesley delivered "An Address to the Clergy," which future pastors today ought to read as a part of their training. In discussing what sort of abilities a minister ought to have, Wesley distinguished between "natural gifts" and "acquired abilities." It is extremely instructive to look at the abilities Wesley thought a minister ought to acquire.

> (1.) Have I such a knowledge of Scripture, as becomes him who undertakes so to explain it to others, that it may be a light in all their paths? . . . Am I acquainted with the several parts of Scripture; with all parts of the Old Testament and the New? Upon the mention of any text, do I know the context, and the parallel places. . . . Do I know the grammatical construction of the four Gospels; of the Acts; of the Epistles; and am I a master of the spiritual sense (as well as the literal) of what I read? . . . Do I know the objections raised to them or from them by Jews, Deists, Papists, Arians, Socinians, and all other sectaries . . . ? Am I ready to give a satisfactory answer to each of these objections?
>
> (2.) Do I understand Greek and Hebrew? Otherwise, how can I undertake (as every minister does), not only to explain books which are written therein, but to defend them against all opponents? Am I not at the mercy of every one who does understand, or even pretends to understand, the original? . . . Do I understand the language of the New Testament? Am I a critical master of it? . . . If not, how many years did I spend at school? How many at the university?

8. Ibib., p. 13.

And what was I doing all those years? Ought not shame to cover my face?

(3.) Do I understand my own office? Have I deeply considered before God the character which I bear? What is it to be an ambassador of Christ, an envoy from the King of heaven?

(4.) Do I understand so much of profane history as tends to confirm and illustrate the sacred? Am I acquainted with the ancient customs of the Jews and other nations mentioned in Scripture? . . . And am I so far (if no farther) skilled in geography, as to know the situation, and give some account, of all the considerable places mentioned therein?

(5.) Am I a tolerable master of the sciences? Have I gone through the very gate of them, logic? If not, I am not likely to go much farther when I stumble at the threshold . . . . Rather, have not my stupid indolence and laziness made me very ready to believe, what the little wits and pretty gentlemen affirm, "that logic is good for nothing"? It is good for this at least . . . , to make people talk less; by showing them both what is, and what is not, to the point; and how extremely hard it is to prove anything. Do I understand metaphysics; if not the depth of the Schoolmen, the subtleties of Scotus or Aquinas, yet the first rudiments, the general principles, of that useful science? Have I conquered so much of it, as to clear my apprehension and range my ideas under proper heads; so much as enables me to read with ease and pleasure, as well as profit, Dr. Henry Moore's Works, Malebranche's "Search After Truth," and Dr. Clark's "Demonstration of the Being and Attributes of God"? Do I understand natural philosophy? If I have not gone deep therein, have I digested the general ground of it? Have I mastered Gravesande, Keill, Sir Isaac Newton's *Principia*, with his "Theory of Light and Colours"? In order thereto, have I laid in some stock of mathematical knowledge? . . . If I have not gone thus far, if I am such a novice still, what have I been about ever since I came from school?

(6.) Am I acquainted with the Fathers; at least with those venerable men who lived in the earliest ages of the Church? Have I read over and over the golden remains of Clemens Romanus, of Ignatius and Polycarp; and have I given one reading, at least, to the works of Justin Martyr, Tertullian, Origen, Clemens Alexandrinus, and Cyprian?

(7.) Have I any knowledge of the world? Have I studied men (as well as books), and observed their tempers,
maxims, and manners? . . . Do I labour never to be rude or
ill mannered; . . . am I . . . affable and courteous to all men?

If I am wanting even in these lowest endowments, shall I
not frequently regret the want? How often shall I . . . be far
less useful than I might have been![9]

Wesley's vision of a pastor is remarkable: a gentleman,
skilled in the Scriptures and conversant with history, philosophy, and the science of his day. How do the pastors
graduating from our seminaries compare to this model?

But finally, it is not just Christian scholars and pastors
who need to be intellectually engaged if the church is to
make an impact in our culture. Christian laymen, too, must
become intellectually engaged. Our churches are filled with
Christians who are idling in intellectual neutral. As Christians, their minds are going to waste.

One result of this is an immature, unreflective faith.
Some people say they prefer having just a "simple faith."
When I was a student at Wheaton College, for example,
one of the graduate students there remarked to me that he
wished in a way that he could return to the simple faith
that the people back in his home church had. His remark
set me back on my heels because it was precisely in order to
have an educated faith that I, as a young Christian, had
come to Wheaton! But after many years of study, I must say
that my attitude is exactly the opposite of my friend's. If a
"simple" faith means an unreflective, ignorant faith, then I
would never go back. For my worship of God is deeper
precisely because of, not in spite of, my philosophical and
theological studies. In every area I have intensely re-
searched—creation, the resurrection, divine omniscience—
my appreciation of God's truth and awe of His person have
become more profound. I am excited about future study
because of the deeper appreciation I am sure it will bring
me of God's person and work. Christian faith is not an

9. John Wesley, *Works* 6:217-31.

apathetic faith, a brain-dead faith, but a living, inquiring faith. As Anselm put it, ours is a faith that seeks understanding.

But the results of being in intellectual neutral extend far beyond one's own self. If Christian laymen do not become intellectually engaged, then we are in serious danger of losing our youth. In high school and college, Christian teenagers are intellectually assaulted by every manner of non-Christian philosophy conjoined with an overwhelming relativism. As I speak in churches around the country, I constantly meet parents whose children have lost their faith because there was no one in the church to answer their questions.

Recently I had the privilege of getting to know Dr. Blanchard Demerchant, now a philosophy professor. Raised in a Christian home, Blanchard began as a teenager to ask questions concerning doubts about the Christian faith that were troubling him. He went away to Bible college, but to his dismay, found that none of the teachers could address his questions. Yet there was in the administration one well-educated man. Demerchant made an appointment with him, hoping to find some answers to his questions. But when Demerchant had laid out his questions, the administrator, instead of dealing with them, merely commanded Demerchant to get down on his knees and repent before God for entertaining such doubts.

Needless to say, that travesty only convinced Demerchant even more that there was nothing intellectually to the Christian faith. He began to study philosophy at a secular university, became an atheist, convinced the Christian girl whom he had married to likewise abandon her faith, was drafted and sent to Vietnam, where he became a drug addict and alcoholic, and later returned to find his marriage, his job, and his world generally falling apart. He nearly committed suicide. But instead, he began to study and ponder the teaching of the man Jesus, and slowly, painfully, he began to return to the Christian faith. To make a long story short, he is now a transformed person, is reunited with his wife, Phyllis, and has a remarkable ministry with secular university students in philosophy by subtly introducing Christian perspective on philosophical problems in the classroom. He told me with a smile that his students are simply dumbfounded that he can be both a philosopher and a Christian. Demerchant's story had a happy ending. But for many other children from Christian families the outcome is far more tragic.

There can be no question that the church has dropped the ball in this area. But the structures are in place in the church for remedying this problem, if only we will make use of them. I am speaking, of course, of adult Sunday school programs. Why not begin to utilize Sunday school classes to offer laymen serious instruction in such subjects as Christian doctrine, church history, New Testament Greek, apologetics, and so forth? Think of the potential for change! Why not?

So if you've been idling intellectually until now, I challenge you to get intellectually engaged. The best way to do this is by reading and taking notes on what you read. To be very practical, I had thought of providing here a list of recommended books in the various areas of biblical studies, doctrine, church history, and apologetics. But the more I thought about it, the more difficult it became to come up with a list that would be applicable to all the different levels at which all of you might be in your Christian education. So instead I suggest that you go to your pastor, tell him you're tired of being in intellectual neutral as a Christian, and ask him to recommend some books that will be appropriate to your level. But give him a minute to think up the list—he'll have to overcome his shock first!

ANSWERS TO THE QUIZ

1. The Roman Catholic monk (1483-1546) who started the Protestant Reformation and was the founder of Lutheranism.

2. The doctrine enunciated at the Council of Chalcedon (451) affirming the true deity and true humanity of Christ.

3. Church Father (354-430) and the author of *The City of God*; he emphasized God's unmerited grace.

4. The church council that in 325 officially ratified the doctrine of the equal deity of the Father and the Son as opposed to the view held by the Arian heretics.

5. The view that the world and God are identical.

6. A medieval Catholic theologian (1225-1274) and the author of *Summa Theologiae*, whose views have been determinative for traditional Roman Catholic theology.

7. The doctrine that in God there are three persons in one being.

8. The origin of Protestantism in the sixteenth century in the efforts of men such as Luther, Calvin, and Zwingli to reform the doctrine and practice of the Roman Catholic church; it emphasized justification by grace through faith alone and the exclusive authority of the Bible.

9. The doctrine that by His death on our behalf and in our place Christ reconciled us to God.

10. The intellectual revolt in Europe during the seventeenth and eighteenth centuries against the authority of church and monarchy in the name of human autonomy; also called the Age of Reason.

1
Doubt

Any Christian who is intellectually engaged and reflecting about his faith will inevitably face the problem of doubt. This problem, I believe, must be very seriously addressed. Too often Christian leaders give lip service to the importance of the mind and the quest after truth, but have a sort of glib confidence that such a quest will invariably wind up at the truth of Christianity. But such a result is by no means guaranteed. During the 1960s, for example, many brilliant students passed through the doors of Wheaton College (Wheaton, Illinois), but those years were also characterized by widespread doubt, cynicism, and unbelief with regard to the faith. I came to Wheaton at the tail end of the sixties, and it troubled me deeply to see some of my classmates, whose intellectual abilities I admired, lose their faith and, to all appearances, reject Christ. This brought home to me in a powerful way how serious the problem of doubt can be.

And yet the church tends to shuffle this problem under the rug. How many sermons have you ever heard on how to deal with doubt in your Christian life? I know of only one book on this subject. Perhaps because Christians aren't supposed to have any doubts, we smile and pretend that this problem doesn't exist. But it does, and nobody is exempt.

A few years ago, for example, while I was on sabbatical at the University of Arizona in Tucson, the pastor of the large Baptist church my wife and I were attending stood up and announced to his congregation that he had experienced a great spiritual victory, which he wanted to share: for the past year he had doubted whether God exists, but now those doubts had been resolved and he felt a new confidence in the Lord! I was so surprised by this admission—who would have thought that this successful pastor of a burgeoning church had doubted that there even is a God? I greatly respected him for his honesty, for what his testimony communicated to his people was that they should not be ashamed of their doubts, when they had them, but could admit them and work through them and seek the help of their pastor, who had walked down that lonely road himself.

A Christian who is thinking for himself will confront doubts; and doubt, if not properly dealt with, can be tremendously destructive of one's spiritual life. You may confront objections to, or intellectual difficulties with, the Christian faith that you cannot answer, and these unanswered questions may lead you to doubt that Christianity is true. Those doubts then begin to gnaw away at the vitality of your spiritual experience: *Maybe it's all an illusion,* you think. *Maybe I'm just kidding myself.* Your devotional life begins to sag and grow dry, for how can you devote yourself to someone who maybe isn't there? Why go on deceiving yourself? That feeling then deadens you to speaking of Christ to others. As one seminary student who was struggling with doubt told me, "How could I tell someone else to receive Christ when I wasn't even sure myself that it was the truth?"

Pretty soon you're on a downward spiral you can't seem to stop. But externally you continue to put on a good face and go to church. You can't admit your doubts to others—what would they think? And so a sort of secret battle rages within, destroying your spiritual life from the inside out, leaving you an empty shell. To make matters worse, you sense your own hypocrisy, and this only serves to add the burden of guilt to the load of doubt you already bear. What can be done? Is there any antidote to doubt?

Well, to begin with, we have to admit that there are no

easy answers to the problem of doubt. There is no simple, quick recipe that if followed will make your doubts vanish like magic. You will probably have to work through your doubts in a slow and agonizing process. You may have to endure what saints have called "the midnight of the soul," or "the dark valley," before coming into the light again; but be assured that many, many great men and women of God have traveled that same path before you and have emerged victorious at the end. Your struggle is not unique, and there is hope of a happy ending.

But what can you do to speed your journey along that path, or better, to avoid it? Let me make four practical suggestions.

First, recognize that doubt is never a purely intellectual problem. There is a spiritual dimension to the problem that must be recognized. Never lose sight of the fact that you are involved in a spiritual warfare and that there is an enemy of your soul who hates you intensely, whose goal is your destruction, and who will stop at nothing to destroy you. Paul reminds us that "our struggle is not against flesh and blood, but against the rulers, against the authorities, against the powers of this dark world and against the spiritual forces of evil in the heavenly realms" (Ephesians 6:12). Doubt is not just a matter of academic debate or disinterested intellectual discussion; it involves a battle for your very soul, and if Satan can use doubt to immobilize you or destroy you, then he will.

Unfortunately, the spiritual dimension inherent in the problem of doubt is often ignored by those involved in higher learning. When I was at Wheaton College, an attitude was prevalent among the students that doubt was actually a virtue and that a Christian who did not doubt his faith was somehow intellectually deficient or naive. But that attitude was unbiblical and confused. It is unbiblical to think of doubt as a virtue; to the contrary, doubt is always portrayed in the Scriptures as something detrimental to spiritual life. Doubt never builds up; it always destroys. How could the students I knew at Wheaton College have got things so totally reversed? It is probably because they had confused *thinking* about their faith with *doubting* their faith. Thinking about your faith is, indeed, a virtue, for it helps you to better understand and defend your faith. But thinking about your faith is not equivalent to doubting your faith.

We need to keep the distinction clear. A student came up to me once after one of my lectures and said, "How come everything you say confirms what my pastor has always taught?" Somewhat amazed, I laughed and said, "Why shouldn't it?" He replied, "Well, all of the other men in the department challenge my faith." My response was, "Look, I don't want to challenge your *faith;* I want to challenge your *thinking.* But I want to *build up* your faith."

My experience as a young Christian of seeing some of my college classmates lose their faith left a deep impression on me, and when I began teaching I resolved to do all I could to help my students stay in the faith while still exploring the intellectual issues about the faith. In particular, I resolved never to present objections to Christianity without also presenting and defending various solutions to those objections. One of my colleagues who did not follow this method was causing some concern among certain Christian students in his classes. "I was only trying to get them to think," he explained to me. "I was just playing the devil's advocate."

Those words hit me like a dash of cold water. For him they were merely a manner of speaking, but it was their literal sense that struck me. *Playing the devil's advocate.* Think of it: to be Satan's advocate in the classroom! That is something we must never allow ourselves to become. As Christian teachers, students, and lay persons, we must never lose sight of the wider spiritual battle in which we are all involved and so must be extremely wary of what we say or write, lest we become the instruments of Satan in destroying someone else's faith. We can challenge people to think more deeply and rigorously about their Christian faith without encouraging them to doubt their faith.

Of course, in thinking about your faith, you are going

to confront difficulties or objections that may cause doubt. But the first point I am trying to emphasize is that when that happens, don't be deceived into thinking that this is merely an intellectual struggle; there is a deeper spiritual dimension to it as well. "Be self-controlled and alert," Peter warns, for "your enemy the devil prowls around like a roaring lion looking for someone to devour" (1 Peter 5:8). Don't be so naive as to think that the devil isn't involved in the intellectual arena, too. We must be ever vigilant, as Paul says, "in order that Satan might not outwit us. For we are not unaware of his schemes" (2 Corinthians 2:11). In particular, Paul warns us not to let anyone make a prey of us "through hollow and deceptive philosophy, which depends on human tradition and the basic principles of this world rather than on Christ" (Colossians 2:8).

When doubts come, then, don't try to hide them or pretend they don't exist. Take them to God in prayer and ask Him to help you resolve them. Tell Him honestly that, say, you doubt His existence, or His being in Christ, or whatever doubt you may have. He cares for you and will help you. I love the prayer of the man who came to Jesus and cried, "I do believe; help me overcome my unbelief!" (Mark 9:24). And what a comfort it is to know that Jesus accepted such a prayer and such faith and responded positively to it! When we have intellectual doubts, that is the time as never before to deepen our spiritual lives and seek the fullness of God's Spirit.

Second, when doubts arise, keep in mind the proper relationship between faith and reason. The question here is, How do I know that my faith is true? Do I know it on the basis of reason? Or do I know its truth by faith itself? Or is my faith founded on authority, or perhaps on mystical experience? How do I know that my Christian faith is true?

As I read the New Testament, the answer is that we know our faith is true by the self-authenticating witness of the Holy Spirit within us. What do I mean by that? I mean that we do not *infer* that our faith is true based on any sort of evidence or proof, but that in the context of the Spirit of

God speaking to our hearts, we *see* immediately and unmis-
takably that our faith is true. God's Spirit makes it evident
to us that our faith is true.

Look briefly with me at what the apostles Paul and
John had to say about this matter. According to Paul, every
Christian is indwelt with the Holy Spirit, and it is the
witness of the Spirit that gives us assurance of being God's
children: "For you did not receive a spirit that makes you a
slave again to fear, but you received the Spirit of sonship.
And by him we cry, '*Abba*, Father.' The Spirit Himself
testifies with our spirit that we are God's children" (Romans 8:15-16). Elsewhere, Paul speaks of this assurance as
"the full riches of complete understanding" (Colossians 2:2)
and as "deep conviction" (1 Thessalonians 1:5). Sometimes
we call this experience "assurance of salvation." Now, clearly, salvation entails that God exists, that Christ atoned for
our sins, that He rose from the dead, and so forth, so that if
you are assured of your salvation, then you must be assured
of all these other truths as well. Hence, the witness of the
Holy Spirit gives the believer an immediate assurance that
his faith is true.

The apostle John teaches the same thing and explicitly
contrasts this assurance with an assurance based on evidence and argument. He begins with a reminder to his
Christian readers: "But you have an anointing from the
Holy One, and all of you know the truth. . . . As for you,
the anointing you received from him remains in you, and
you do not need anyone to teach you. But as his anointing
teaches you about all things and as that anointing is real,
not counterfeit—just as it has taught you, remain in him"
(1 John 2:20). Here the anointing of the Holy Spirit, which
every Christian enjoys, is the source of our knowing the
truth about our faith. John then goes on to contrast the
confidence the Spirit of God brings with the assurance
brought by human evidence: "For there are three that testify: the Spirit, the water and the blood; and the three are
in agreement. We accept man's testimony, but God's testimony is greater because it is the testimony of God, which
he has given about his Son. Anyone who believes in the

Son of God has this testimony in his heart" (1 John 5:7-10a). The "water" here probably refers to Jesus' baptism, and the "blood" to His crucifixion, those two events being the ones that marked the beginning and the end of His earthly ministry. "Man's testimony" is therefore nothing less than the apostolic testimony to the events of Jesus' life and ministry. Yet John declares that even though we quite rightly receive this testimony, still the inner testimony of the Holy Spirit is greater. Such a statement is remarkable because in his gospel, John had laid great weight precisely on the apostolic testimony: "these [signs] are written that you may believe that Jesus is the Christ, the Son of God. . . . This is the disciple who testifies to these things and who wrote them down. We know that his testimony is true" (John 20:31; 21:24). But here in his first epistle he asserts that the knowledge inspired by the Holy Spirit is even more certain than the testimony of the apostles themselves.

The view of the New Testament, then, is that fundamentally we know our faith to be true by the self-authenticating witness of God's Holy Spirit.

What role, then, is left for reason to play? Here I think a distinction made by the Protestant Reformer Martin Luther can be of help. Luther distinguished between what he called the *magisterial* and the *ministerial* uses of reason. In the magisterial use of reason, reason sits over and above the gospel like a magistrate and judges whether it is true or false. In the ministerial use of reason, reason submits to and serves the gospel as a handmaiden. Luther maintained that only the ministerial use of reason is legitimate, and from what I have just said, we can see that he was right. It is a usurpation of the role properly belonging to the Holy Spirit Himself for reason to assume the magisterial role. For it is the Holy Spirit who teaches us directly the truth of the gospel, and reason has no right to contradict Him.

Instead, reason's role is that of a servant. Reason is a God-given instrument to help us better understand and defend our faith. Though the Holy Spirit gives us assurance of the basic truth of our faith, He does not impart knowledge of all its ramifications and ins and outs—for example, whether God is timeless or everlasting, how to reconcile providence and free will, or how to formulate the doctrine of the Trinity. Those are things we must decide by thinking about them.

As Anselm put it, ours is a faith that seeks understanding. In a similar way, reason can be used to defend our faith by formulating arguments for the existence of God or refuting objections. But though the arguments so developed serve to confirm the truth of our faith, they are not properly the basis of our faith, for that is supplied by the witness of the Holy Spirit Himself. Even if there were no arguments in defense of the faith, our faith would still have its firm foundation.

Now what is the implication of all this for the problem of doubt? Simply this: *doubt is controllable so long as reason does not usurp the magisterial role.* So long as reason operates in its ministerial role, the spiritual assurance of our faith cannot be undermined. It is only when we allow reason to usurp the magisterial role and take the place of the Holy Spirit that doubt becomes dangerous.

That is not to say that Christianity cannot stand up to reason. On the contrary, I believe that someone who had all the facts and never made a mistake would, if he followed the magisterial role of reason, conclude that Christianity is true. Of course, such a person would also be God and therefore hardly need any proof. But the point is that people in different times and places and with differing abilities and opportunities do not have all the facts and do make errors in reasoning. In certain historical circumstances, the evidence available may be against Christianity. If persons in those situations repressed and ignored the witness of the Holy Spirit and followed instead the magisterial role of reason, they would be led to unbelief.

On the other hand, if we attend to the witness of the Spirit and do not allow reason to transgress its proper function, then we shall not lose faith even when we are confronted with objections that we, with our limited abilities, cannot refute. Alvin Plantinga, a great Christian philosopher, provides a helpful illustration of what I mean.

I am applying to the National Endowment for the Humanities for a fellowship, I write a letter to a colleague, trying to bribe him to write the Endowment a glowing letter on my behalf; he indignantly refuses and sends the letter to my chairman. The letter disappears from the chairman's office under mysterious circumstances. I have a motive for stealing it; I have the opportunity to do so; and I have been known to do such things in the past. Furthermore, an extremely reliable member of the department claims to have seen me furtively entering the chairman's office at about the time when the letter must have been stolen. The evidence against me is very strong; my colleagues reproach me for such underhanded behavior and treat me with evident distaste. The facts of the matter, however, are that I didn't steal the letter and in fact spent the entire afternoon in question on a solitary walk in the woods; furthermore, I clearly remember spending that afternoon walking in the woods.

In such a case, all the evidence stands against me and yet I know I am not guilty. For the evidence cannot overcome the more basic knowledge I have of the truth of my innocence. Even if the evidence is irrefutable, such that others ought to think me guilty, I myself am not obliged to go along with the evidence, for I know better.[1]

In the same way, given the witness of the Spirit in my life, giving me an immediate assurance of the truth of my faith, I needn't be shaken when objections come along that I can't answer. For I have a foundation for my faith that is deeper and more sure than the shifting sands of evidence and argument.

The point is this: the secret to dealing with doubt in the Christian life is not to resolve all of one's doubts, for that is probably impossible in a finite lifetime. One will always have unanswered questions. Rather, the secret is learning to live victoriously with one's unanswered questions. By understanding the true foundation of our faith and by assigning to reason its proper role, we can prevent unanswered questions from turning into destructive

1. Alvin Plantinga, "The Foundations of Theism: A Reply," *Faith and Philosophy* 3 (1986):310.

doubts. In such a case, we shall not have answers to all our questions, but in a deeper sense that will not matter. For we will know that our faith is true on the basis of the Spirit's witness, and we can live confidently even while having questions we cannot answer. That is why it is so important to keep in mind the proper relationship between faith and reason.

Third, remember the frailty of our limited intellects and knowledge. Socrates said that he was the wisest man in Athens because he knew that he knew nothing. The apostle Paul, when confronted with Greek Gnostics, who touted the importance of knowledge, took a similar line. "Knowledge," he wrote, "puffs up, but love builds up. The man who thinks he knows something does not yet know as he ought to know. But the man who loves God is known by God" (1 Corinthians 8:1b-3). According to Paul, if you think you're so smart that you've got it all figured out about God, then in fact you don't know anything. You're just an inflated intellectual blowhard. By contrast, the person who loves God is the one who truly has come to know Him.

Such a doctrine has shattering implications for our proud intellectual attainments. It means that the simplest child of God who lives in love is wiser in God's sight than the most brilliant Bertrand Russell the world has ever seen.

We as Christians need to realize the feebleness and finitude of our human knowledge. I can honestly testify that the more I learn, the more desperately ignorant I feel. Further study only serves to open up to one's consciousness all the endless vistas of knowledge, even in one's own field, about which one knows absolutely nothing. I can identify with a statement Isaac Newton made at the end of his great treatise on physics, the *Principia.* He said that he felt like a little child playing with pretty pebbles on the seashore while the great ocean of truth stretched away all undiscovered before him. How feeble, uncertain, and unstable are our intellectual attainments!

When my wife and I were studying in England, I visited the great historian of philosophy, Frederick C. Copleston, in London. He had spent his entire life writing a massive, nine-volume *History of Philosophy* from the ancient Greeks through the twentieth century, as well as numerous works on such subjects as Oriental philosophy and Russian philosophy. I asked him if, after this lifetime of study, he had learned some overriding lesson from the history of philosophy. He replied that he had and then explained that when he started the project, he had hoped to show that the philosophy of Thomas Aquinas was the age-lasting philosophy. But it soon became evident to him that it was impossible to do that. Instead, what his study of the history of thought had shown him, he said, was how bound any man's philosophy is to the day and age in which he lives, to the thought-forms of his era and culture, to the intellectual milieu in which he writes. That did not mean that Copleston was a relativist; it meant that we have to be very cautious in our claims to have discovered some truth and very modest about our own intellectual attainments.

What application does Copleston's point have to the problem of doubt? It means that we should be cautious, indeed, about thinking that we have come upon the decisive disproof of our faith. It is pretty unlikely that we have found the irrefutable objection. The history of philosophy is littered with the wrecks of such objections. Given the confidence that the Holy Spirit inspires, we should esteem lightly the arguments and objections that generate our doubts.

I shudder when I read the words of certain non-Christian philosophers who solemnly claim to have proved, say, that God cannot be omnipotent, or that God cannot be omniscient, or that miracles are impossible, or some such dogmatic assertion. Some time ago I read an article by a philosopher who claimed to have proved that God cannot know that He is God! The problem with such an article is not just that its conclusion is based on a ludicrously fallacious argument. The point is rather that the article is in a real sense blasphemous. It represents philosophy at its worst, the sort Paul warned against in Colossians 2:8. If with our limited intellects and resources we cannot discover the resolution to some objection or to an apparent antinomy, such as that, say, between the concept of divine foreknowledge and the concept of human freedom, rather than doubt or deny the Christian faith at that point, we ought simply to hold the truth in tension and admit that the difficulty lies in our own lack of insight into the problem and its solution. We need to remember the frailty of our limited intellects and knowledge.

Fourth, pursue your doubts into the ground. We have seen that the secret to handling doubt in our lives is not to resolve every question but *to learn to live victoriously with unresolved questions.* Any thinking Christian will have a "question bag" filled with unresolved difficulties he must learn to live with. But from time to time, as you have opportunity, it's good to take the bag down from the shelf, select one of the questions, and go to work on answering it. Indeed, I can say that working hard on an unresolved question and pursuing it until you finally find an answer that satisfies you intellectually is one of the most exhilarating experiences of the Christian life. To resolve a doubt that has troubled you for some time brings a wonderful sense of intellectual peace and inspires confidence that there are solutions to the remaining difficulties in your question bag.

When you have a doubt about or a question about a particular area, set aside time to study that area by reading books or articles on the subject. Libraries at Christian colleges or seminaries can be particularly helpful, if those are available where you live. Even public libraries can order what you need through their interlibrary loan service. Find out what Christian scholars have written in the area you are exploring and write to them—or, if possible, visit them to discuss your question. Seek out and talk with those members of the Body of Christ who have studied the subject.

In that way, the members of the Body will be helping to build each other up. But don't let your doubts just sit there: pursue them and keep after them until you drive them into the ground.

Doubt can be an agonizing experience in the Christian life, and there is no "quick fix" for resolving it. It requires patience and endurance. But I believe you will find the four points I've mentioned helpful in handling doubt.

May God give us by the Holy Spirit the gift of faith that we may triumph over doubt and take every thought captive to obey Christ.

2

Unanswered Prayer

"Whatever you ask in My name, I will do it," Jesus promised. In fact, Jesus repeated this promise three times in different words in John 14, 15, and 16. "And I will do whatever you ask in my name" (John 14:13a); "then the Father will give you whatever you ask in my name" (15:16); "if you ask anything of the Father, He will give it to you in my name" (16:23b). Jesus evidently really meant business. That is a wonderful, astounding claim.

But the problem is that this promise just does not seem to be unqualifiedly true. Often the preacher may exhort us to lay hold of the promise in our personal lives, to believe it and claim it for ourselves. But the problem is that we *can't* believe the promise because it is simply unbelievable in its unqualified form. For if we are ruthlessly honest with ourselves, every one of us knows that sometimes God does not answer our prayers.

Indeed, sometimes He *cannot* answer our prayers because Christians are praying for contradictory things. When I was a student at Wheaton, I heard about two guys who were both in love with the same girl. Each one was praying that God would turn her affections toward him so that he might marry her. Now clearly the prayers of at least one of those young men was going to be unanswered. God couldn't answer them both because their prayers were contradictory. Or imagine two Christian athletes playing on opposite sides in the Superbowl or in the World Series. Each would naturally be disposed to pray that his team would win, and yet both prayers could not be answered, for the two athletes would be praying for contradictory results.

But on an even more everyday level, every one of us has experienced unanswered prayer. We have asked God to do something, something we think will glory Him, and we have prayed in faith believing—and God didn't come through. Sometimes unanswered prayer of this kind involves cases of prayer for healing. One church I knew of prayed for the miraculous healing of one of its members. The people really believed God and were expecting a miracle. But the man died. Many people were deeply shaken in their Christian faith; they had asked God in faith for something in Jesus' name and He did not do it. Perhaps Jesus' promise was not true after all—maybe the Christian faith was not true after all.

And it's not just Christian laymen who confront this problem. Christian spiritual leaders also experience unanswered prayer. I once heard Cliff Barrows say that his partners on the Billy Graham team had long ago ceased to pray for good weather for their crusades—indeed, some of their best crusades have been held in the rain. In his Youth Seminars Bill Gothard tells one incredible story after another about how God brought in the money to pay the bills, but he also admits, "In all fairness to God, He did not always come through in the nick of time." In other words, some prayers went unanswered.

Now someone might say, "But you can't use human experience to qualify God's promises!" But the problem with this response is that the Scriptures themselves gives examples of unanswered prayer. Think of Paul's so-called "thorn in the flesh"—a physical ailment he asked God three times to remove (2 Corinthians 12:7). But God did not. Paul also asked the Roman church to pray that he might be delivered from the unbelievers in Jerusalem on what turned out to be his final visit there (Romans 15:31). But he was not delivered; instead we read in Acts 21 of Paul's arrest in Jerusalem and the imprisonment that eventually led to his martyrdom. So even the Scriptures themselves give examples of unanswered prayer. It is not unqualifiedly true that whatever we ask in Jesus' name we shall receive.

But this is very troubling. For Jesus promised that whatever we asked in His name we would receive. So is His promise empty? Worse still, how can Jesus be God if He makes empty promises? How does one solve the problem of unanswered prayer?

First, let's look at inadequate solutions to this problem that are often used by Christians today. One solution is simply to deny that prayer ever goes unanswered. This is the most radical solution, and yet it is sometimes espoused by well-meaning Christians. For example, when my wife, Jan, and I were on Campus Crusade staff at Northern Illinois University our movement was infiltrated by certain Christians who believed that physical healing was included in the atonement of Christ, and thus no Christian ever needed to be sick. Just pray to God and He will heal you!

Well, the result of this was that some of our students were throwing away their glasses, claiming that they were healed, even though they couldn't see any better. I remember confronting one of them by asking, "Are you healed?" He said, "Yes, I am." So I said, "Well, can you see any better?" "No," he admitted. "So then how are you healed if you can't see any better?" I asked. "Because my faith isn't strong enough," he said. "I am healed, but I just don't have faith to believe it." And so these poor, nearsighted students were going around trying to study and attend classes without their glasses, claiming that they were healed but that they lacked the faith to believe that God had answered their prayers. I wonder what those Christians would say about someone who died from cancer despite prayers for healing: that he really was alive and well but just appeared to be dead because he lacked the faith? What those Christians needed was not more faith, but some common sense!

A less radical, but nevertheless inadequate, solution often proposed is that God always answers prayer, but that His answers may vary between yes, no, and wait. Thus, a prayer that receives a negative answer is not really an unanswered prayer. God *did* answer, namely, by saying no. But this solution is just playing at words. What we mean by unanswered prayer is prayer that receives a negative answer. Jesus promised that whatever we ask in His name we shall receive. It does nothing to solve the problem for someone to say that God *did* answer your prayer but said no, for the promise is that He will always say yes. So the problem remains the same just under different words, namely, how can there be negatively answered prayer?

A third inadequate solution that Christians sometimes use is to rationalize things away so that they can say God answered the prayer after all. Once I was at a meeting where prayer was offered for God to help a seriously ill man get out of the hospital. But the following day the man died. At the next meeting the speaker who had led in prayer the night before announced the man's death and proclaimed triumphantly that our prayers had been answered. "We asked God to take him out of the hospital, and praise the Lord, He has!" Well, this sort of rationalization strikes me as basically dishonest. It was clear that the intent of our prayers the night before was that God would heal the man. Rationalizing away a negative answer to prayer is to view God as a great genie from Aladdin's lamp who fulfills the technical language of our requests but misses the intent altogether, so that we wind up with something totally different from what we requested. That is not the God of the Bible. Why not be honest and admit that God just did not answer the prayer?

So I think a proper solution lies in a different direction. I do not think that Jesus' promise is empty, but I do think that it must be qualified. It is not true simply and without qualification that you will receive whatever you ask in Jesus' name. The promise must be qualified in certain ways in accordance with the teaching of the rest of Scripture.

Now qualifying the promise may sound distressing to you, but let me point out that there are precedents for doing so. Other teachings of Jesus also have to be qualified in light of different Scriptures. Take Jesus' teachings on divorce, for example. In Mark 10:11, Jesus makes the blanket statement, "Anyone who divorces his wife and marries another woman commits adultery against her." No exception is allowed. But in Matthew 19:9 Jesus says, "I tell you that anyone who divorces his wife, except for marital unfaithfulness, and marries another woman commits adultery." Here the former statement is qualified: there is an exception which permits divorce after all, namely, marital unfaithfulness on the part of a spouse. Now I'm suggesting that Jesus' promises about prayer also need to be qualified in this way. Implicit in Jesus' blanket promise are certain important qualifiers, and if those qualifiers are not met, one cannot claim the promise.

What are some of those implicit qualifications to Jesus' promise? Many of them can be classed under the heading "Obstacles to Answered Prayer." Let's look at some of them.

1. *Sin in our lives.* The most basic and, I think, prevalent obstacle to answered prayer is unconfessed sin in our lives. Jesus' promise naturally presupposes that the person praying is a Christian living in the fullness and power of the Holy Spirit. A Christian who is living in unconfessed sin or in the power of the flesh can have no confidence that his prayers will be answered. The psalmist said, "If I had cherished sin in my heart, the Lord would not have listened" (Psalm 66:18). In what must be a terribly convicting verse to us married men, Peter writes that husbands should live considerately with their wives, bestowing honor on the physically weaker sex, in order that their prayers may not be hindered (see 1 Peter 3:7). Think of it: not treating your wife right hinders your prayers! Jesus' promise assumes that the believer is abiding in Christ, keeping His commandments, walking in the light, filled with the Spirit, and loving the brethren. When you think about this, it's only by God's grace that any of our prayers are answered!

2. *Wrong motives.* Many times our prayers go unanswered because our motives are wrong. Too often, our prayers are motivated by selfishness—a sort of "Gimme,

gimme, gimme" attitude centered wholly on ourselves. Jesus had promised, "Ask and it will be given to you" (Matthew 7:7), but James explained to his readers, "When you ask, you do not receive, because you ask with wrong motives, that you may spend what you get on your pleasures" (James 4:3). Prayer that is totally self-centered does not fall under Jesus' promise.

I remember seeing a tract on why there is no revival in the church today. One of the reasons was depicted in a cartoon labeled "A Modern Saint Struggles with the Forces of Darkness." It was a picture of a man kneeling by his bedside contending with God in prayer: "Oh Lord, *please* give us that new color television set! You know how much we need it. Please, Lord, please, help us get that color TV!" The correct motive for our prayer requests should be God's glory. Hence, in the Old Testament one often finds prayers based on the desire that God would do some act for the sake of His name. It was Jesus' prayer that God would glorify His name (see John 12:28). This should be our motive in prayer: to request things of God, not that our selfish desires might be satisfied, but that His name might be glorified.

3. *Lack of faith.* Jesus Himself made clear that only believing prayer can be assured of an answer. He told the disciples, "Whatever you ask for in prayer, believe that you have received it, and it will be yours" (Mark 11:24). Here the promise is qualified such that prayer must be accompanied by faith. If you have faith that God will answer your request and you do not doubt, then He will answer it. By contrast, the man who is ridden by doubts cannot have any confidence that his prayer will be answered. Thus, James says, speaking of a man's prayers for wisdom, "When he asks, he must believe and not doubt, because he who doubts is like a wave of the sea, blown and tossed by the wind. That man should not think he will receive anything from the Lord; he is a double-minded man, unstable in all he does" (James 1:6-8).

Of course, this statement raises all sorts of difficult

questions about how one acquires that kind of faith and how such a faith can be sustained in the face of unanswered prayer. I'm not going to try to treat such questions now. Let me just note that Jesus also said that the faith required need not be great, but that mighty things can happen as a result of faith as small as a grain of mustard seed (see Luke 17:6); and let us also remember that faith is a gift of God. We can always pray, "Lord, I believe! Help thou mine unbelief!" (Mark 9:24, KJV*). In any case, my main point here is that one more qualification must be introduced into Jesus' promise: we must pray in faith.

4. *Lack of earnestness.* Sometimes our prayers are not answered because, quite frankly, we don't really care whether they are. We casually pray in the prayer meeting for some request and then forget all about it. We hardly ever think to ask later how that prayer was answered. We don't really care. That's why when Jan and I were involved raising financial support to go to Europe, we were pretty unimpressed when someone said, "I'll pray for you." Usually what that really meant was "I'm not interested enough to support you financially." But if that's true, then I honestly doubt that he's interested enough to pray earnestly, either.

Unfortunately, Christians have the idea that prayer support is a lesser commitment than financial support, when in reality precisely the opposite is the case. It doesn't take much effort to write a check every month or so and never think of it again, but it's tough to pray earnestly and regularly for a missionary or Christian worker. But it is precisely this earnest prayer, this serious, heartfelt, get-down-to-business-with-God prayer, that God attends to. Read the great prayers of the Bible and ask yourself if those people were earnest or not. A beautiful example is Hannah's prayer for a son in 1 Samuel 1. She was so intense in her prayer, so oblivious to everything going on around her, that the priest at the house of the Lord thought she was drunk! But of course the supreme example was Jesus Him-

* King James Version.

self, a man who would continue all night in prayer to God, who literally wore the disciples out by having them pray with Him. Read Jesus' prayers in the gospels and ask if this man was not earnestly involved in His praying. Our prayers may often go unanswered because we really care so little.

5. *Lack of perseverance.* Closely related to earnestness is perseverance in prayer. Our lack of persistence may be one reason our prayers are not answered. We give up so easily. We pray once or twice, and then we're through. Some Christians will tell you that all you have to do is pray once about something, commit it to the Lord, and then relax and trust Him to take care of it. But I think I can say confidently that this is not the teaching of Jesus. Think of the parable of the friend coming at midnight to borrow some bread from his neighbor (Luke 11:5-8). The neighbor won't get up out of bed at first, but because his friend keeps pounding at the door and won't go away, he gets up and gives him the bread. How much more, says Jesus, will your heavenly Father give to you!

Or think of the parable of the widow and the judge (Luke 18:1-8). The unrighteous judge did not want to grant the woman's request, but she kept pestering him so much he said he would grant her request or else "she will wear me out by her continual coming" (18:5b, RSV*). The point of the parable, says Luke, is that "we should always pray and not give up" (18:1). If we want something bad enough, we should beat a path to heaven's door and make its portals ring with our continual pounding. In Jan's and my own experience, some of our most dramatic answers to prayer— like getting a two-year fellowship from the West German government to study the evidence for the resurrection— have come as a response to prayers offered morning and evening over a period of several months. Don't give up too soon in your prayer for something. Show God that you mean business.

These, then, are some of the obstacles to answered

* *Revised Standard Version.*

prayer: *sin in our lives, wrong motives, lack of faith, lack of earnestness, lack of perseverance.* If any of those obstacles hinders our prayers, then we cannot claim with confidence Jesus' promise "Whatever you ask in my name, I will do it" (John 14:13*a*, RSV).

But, of course, this isn't the end of the story. For the frustrating thing about unanswered prayer is that on occasion none of the obstacles just listed seems to impede the way, and still God does not grant our request. We may have confessed all known sin in our lives, prayed out of a desire to glorify God, and prayed in faith with earnestness and perseverance, and still God doesn't come through as Jesus said He would. Indeed, it is precisely when all those elements are present that the experience of unanswered prayer is apt to be devastating and demoralizing.

There is, however, one final, important qualification of Jesus' promise that needs to be made: our request must be in accordance with God's will. The apostle John makes this clear in 1 John 5:14-15: "This is the confidence we have in approaching God: that if we ask anything according to his will, he hears us. And if we know that he hears us—whatever we ask—we know that we have what we asked of him." It may well be the case that sometimes our prayers are not answered, not due to some fault of our own, but simply because God knows better than we do what ought to be done. Our perspective and wisdom are limited, but God's is the viewpoint of omniscience. He knows, as we do not, that sometimes it is better not to grant our requests.

Notice that John says our confidence is that if our prayers are in accordance with God's will, He will answer them. Therefore, we should always temper our prayers with the attitude "If it be Thy will." Now very often you hear it said that to pray "If it be Thy will" is a sort of namby-pamby, Milquetoast kind of prayer that shows a lack of boldness before God. I don't think the Scripture supports that assertion. John says that our confidence is not that God will answer our prayers, but that He will answer our prayers if they are in accordance with His will. Our degree of confidence that He will answer our prayers is proportional to our degree of confidence that they are His will. If we aren't sure our requests express His will, it is entirely proper to say, "If it be Thy will."

The decisive vindication of this way of praying is that this is the way Jesus prayed. In the Garden of Gethsemane He asked that God would avert the crucifixion, but then He added, "Yet not my will, but yours be done" (Luke 22:42). To ask for God's will is an expression of humility and submission to God. It is to acknowledge that He knows better than we do, and that we want His will even more than we want our request. When Paul prayed that God would heal him of his thorn in the flesh, God declined his request, saying, "My grace is sufficient for you, for my power is made perfect in weakness" (2 Corinthians 12:9a). Paul's response? "I will boast all the more gladly about my weakness, so that Christ's power may rest upon me. That is why, for Christ's sake, I delight in weaknesses, in insults, in hardships, in persecutions, in difficulties. For when I am weak, then I am strong" (12:9b-10). Paul wanted to be healed, yes, but even more he wanted God's will for his life. Our attitude should be the same.

If we want our prayers to be answered, we should pray in accordance with God's will. But how do we know what sorts of things represent His will? Well, perhaps the best way to discern that is to read the prayers of the Bible to see what great men of God prayed for. I think we might be a little surprised. Read the prayers of Paul in his epistles, for example.

In *Ephesians*, Paul prayed:
　　　that God would give the Ephesians a spirit of wisdom in the knowledge of Himself
　　　that they would know
　　　　　the hope to which they had been called
　　　　　the riches of God's inheritance in the saints
　　　　　the greatness of God's power
　　　that they would be strengthened through the Holy Spirit in the inner self
　　　　that Christ would dwell in their hearts by faith
　　　　that they, being rooted in love, would have the ability

to know Christ's unfathomable love, so that they might be filled with all God's fullness.

In *Philippians*, Paul prayed:

that the Philippians' love would abound more and more, coupled with knowledge and discernment, so that they would approve what is excellent and be pure and blameless at Christ's return, filled with the fruits of righteousness.

In *Colossians*, Paul prayed:

that the Colossians would be filled with the knowledge of God's will in all spiritual wisdom and understanding, so that they would lead a life worthy of the Lord, fully pleasing to Him, bearing fruit in every good work, and increasing in the knowledge of God.

In the letters to the *Thessalonians*, Paul asked:

that the Lord would make the Thessalonians increase and abound in love toward one another and toward all men, so that they would be established unblamable in holiness at Christ's return

that the Lord would comfort their hearts and establish them in every good work and deed.

And in the letter to *Philemon*, Paul prayed:

that the sharing of Philemon's faith would promote the knowledge of all the good that is ours in Christ.

Are *those* the kind of things for which you pray? Why not?

I suspect that very often we are praying for the wrong things. What we desire is not what God desires, and so our prayers go askew. Our prayers will be answered only as our desires are brought into line with His.

Now two objections might be raised at this point. First, it might be said that we have so qualified Jesus' original promise that it has suffered death by a thousand qualifications. For there is an enormous difference between saying, "Whatever you ask in my name, I will do it," and saying, "Whatever you ask in name, if you have no unconfessed sin in your life, and your motives are pure, and you have faith, and you are really in earnest, and you persist in asking, and, to top it all off, if it is God's will, then I will do it." I feel the force of this objection, but in the end I do not think it will stand. For I feel sure that when Jesus made that original promise, He naturally presupposed the qualifications we have just listed and would agree to them if we could ask Him today. Indeed, most of those qualifications come from His own teachings, as we have seen.

As for the stipulation concerning God's will, His blanket promise is not incompatible with this qualification. For example, John, who in 1 John 5:14 makes the qualification that prayer should be in accordance with God's will, made just a few paragraphs earlier a blanket promise almost like the one Jesus made: "Dear friends, if our hearts do not condemn us, we have confidence before God and receive from him anything we ask, because we obey his commands and do what pleases him" (1 John 3:21-22). Thus, in the course of a single letter John says that if our lives are pleasing to God, we receive whatever we ask (3:21-22), *and* that if we ask anything according to His will, we receive whatever we ask (5:14). John did not think the qualification in 5:14 nullified the promise made in 3:21-22. Why should Jesus have thought any differently?

And when you reflect on it, it would be a recipe for disaster for God to simply give us whatever we ask. For we would always pray to be delivered from any suffering or trial, and yet we know from Scripture that suffering builds character and trials perfect our faith. If God gave us whatever we asked, we would be immature, spoiled children, not men and women of God. On the other hand, I think John may also be saying that as we keep Christ's commands and grow into His likeness, our wills come to coincide more and more with God's will, so that we can have confidence that whatever we ask we shall receive. But even the most Christlike saint, even Christ Himself, because of our limited perspective, must sometimes pray, "Not my will, but Thine be done."

A second objection is to say that when we pray, "Thy will be done," Jesus' promise to answer our prayers becomes unfalsifiable. That is to say, there is no way to tell if His promise is really true, for any time we pray for something and do not receive it, we can always say, "It wasn't God's will"! Therefore, the promise seems empty. But this objection betrays a lack of understanding as to how we know that our Christian faith is true. Our confidence in the truth of Christianity in general and Jesus' promise in particular is not based on the evidence of answered prayer. Our confidence in the truth of our faith is based on the witness of the Holy Spirit, confirmed by reason. Prayer is one of the dimensions of the life of faith, not of apologetics. The Christian life is a walk by faith, and it is strictly irrelevant whether God's promises are falsifiable or not. The point is, we think Christianity is true (or presumably we wouldn't have become Christians), and so we place our trust in God's promises. Consequently, the objection is based on a misunderstanding.

But if there are no objections to this understanding of prayer and God's will, there is still a real danger here, which I have experienced, namely, timidity in prayer. That is to say, because we are uncertain of God's will in a specific situation, we do not know what to pray for. So we are afraid to ask God for something, lest we be praying outside His will. If a friend is sick, should we pray that God heal him or that God give him courage and faith in his suffering? If we are unemployed, should we pray for a job or for an attitude of contentment as we learn to be abased? If someone is going through a trial, should we pray for deliverance or steadfastness? We can be so cowed by not knowing what to pray for that we cease to pray, which is certainly not God's will. What are we supposed to do?

Well, praise be to God, there is a ministry of the Holy Spirit especially suited to this problem! Paul addresses precisely this problem in Romans 8:26-27: "In the same way, the Spirit helps us in our weakness. We do not know what we ought to pray for, but the Spirit himself intercedes for us with groans that words cannot express. And he who searches our hearts knows the mind of the Spirit, because the Spirit intercedes for the saints in accordance with God's will." We may not know what to pray for, but the Holy Spirit takes our prayers and translates them, as it were, into

accordance with God's will before the throne of grace.
With such a divine intercessor, we can pray boldly, even
within our limited perspective, confident that the Holy
Spirit is interceding according to the will of God. Therefore, be bold in your prayers and ask Him forthrightly for
what you, using your spiritual wisdom and discernment,
think best. That was also Paul's procedure. He boldly asked
God to heal him, and he frequently asked churches to pray
for his deliverance from persecutors, though in the end
God had a different will for Paul. Pray according to your
wisdom and your heart's desire, and trust the Holy Spirit to
intercede for you according to the will of God.

In conclusion, I think it is obvious that this discussion
has enormous practical implications for our lives. For although we have concentrated on unanswered prayer, since
it is problematic, it is clear from Jesus' promise that un-
answers prayer ought to be the exception, not the norm, of
our prayer life. For the Christian abiding in Christ, answers to his prayers ought to be his regular experience.
Now, how about your prayer life? Are you just muddling
along in the Christian life, never seeing God really work in
response to your prayers? When was the last time you
moved the hands of God through prayer?

If you are not satisfied with your prayer life, maybe it's
time to take inventory of the obstacles to answered prayer
in your life. What is that unconfessed sin, that area of
uncleanness in your life you've been rationalizing away or
hiding from God? What room in your heart has not yet
been opened to Christ and yielded to His lordship? Have
you been praying just for selfish things that you might
spend your passions on them? Or are you really seeking
God's glory? Are you really believing God for answers to
your prayers? Or have you become so accustomed to lack of
answers that you've been lulled into a spiritual lethargy that
expects no answer and so gets no answer from God? Do
you really care whether He answers or not? Do you go to
God with an intense, burning desire to have your requests
from Him? Do you pray once and forget about it, or do you

come to God again and again? Do you wrestle with God, saying with Jacob, "I will not let you go unless you bless me" (Genesis 32:26b)? In a word, do you pray because that's what Christians are expected to do, or do you mean business with God?

If you do, let me make this suggestion: set aside some time tomorrow—or even today—to take inventory of the hindrances to prayer in your life. Repent, ask God's forgiveness, and start anew. Make out a prayer list of specific people and things to pray for on different days of the week, and then set aside time to pray each day for these. Be specific, and put a red check by each request as it is answered. As you see God work, your faith will increase as you learn to trust Him for more.

If you already have a vital prayer life but have been troubled by certain unanswered prayers, you need to trust God for His perfect will. Reflect on His omniscience and His goodness. If you ask Him for bread, will He give you a stone? (Matthew 7:9). If you ask for a fish, will He give you a scorpion? (Luke 11:12). God will give to you what His good and acceptable and perfect will decrees. You may not always get what you ask for, but God knows best what will serve to advance His kingdom. You can trust Him for His answers.

Prayer is hard work. But the promises of prayer are great. Let us therefore strive to lay hold of those promises.

3

Failure

I have been a Christian for some twenty years. I estimate that in my Christian lifetime I have attended upward of twelve hundred church services, three hundred chapels at Wheaton College, and scores of Christian meetings at retreats, conferences, and so on, held by Campus Crusade and other groups. Yet during this entire time I have never once—not a single time in the hundreds of meetings over some twenty-odd years—heard a speaker address the subject of failure. In fact, I probably would not myself have reflected seriously on the topic if it had not been for a crushing failure that drove me to face the problem personally.

The lack of treatment of this subject on the part of Christian speakers is not due to any lack of importance in the subject. Any Christian who has failed at some time knows how devastating the experience can be and the questions it raises: *Where is God? How could He let this happen? Am I outside His will? What do I do now? Does God really care or exist?* Those are agonizing questions. What is the meaning of failure for a Christian?

In addressing this problem, it seems to me that we need first to distinguish two types of failure: *failure in the Christian life* and *failure in the life of a Christian.* By failure in the Christian life, I mean a failure in a believer's relationship and walk with God. For example, a Christian might experience disappointment and failure due to a refusal to heed God's calling, or by succumbing to temptation, or through marrying a non-Christian. Failure of this type is due to sin. It is essentially a spiritual problem, a matter of moral and spiritual failure.

By contrast, failure in the life of a Christian is unrelated to spiritual considerations. It is not due to sin in the life of a believer. It is just some defeat a person who happens to be a Christian experiences in his day-to-day life. For example, a Christian businessman might go bankrupt, a Christian athlete might see his boyhood dreams shattered when he fails to make the major leagues, a Christian student might flunk out of school despite his best efforts to succeed, or a Christian workingman might find himself unemployed and unable to find a job. Such cases are not instances of failure in a person's walk with God but instances of failure in the ordinary course of life. They just happen to occur in the lives of people who are Christians.

In his best-selling book *Failure: The Back Door to Success*, Erwin Lutzer deals with the distinction I am trying to make here. He attributes failure in the Christian life to lust of the flesh (sexual gratification), pride of life (egoism), or lust of the eyes (covetousness). Failure in the life of a Christian that is not related to those elements is just part of life. Lutzer finds no particular difficulty with the second type of failure, but he does find the first kind of failure problematic. He writes:

> What causes failure? What makes a man come to the end of his life and admit he lived in vain? What motivates a man to commit suicide because he is not as gifted as others? . . . What causes a man to jeopardize his Christian testimony and have an affair with his neighbor's wife? The answer: Sin—specifically, pride, covetousness, or sensual desire.
>
> Of course, there are failures quite unrelated to sinful motivations: a student might fail in school, a man might make an unwise investment. Many people have failed at their jobs or simply fallen short of their goals. We shouldn't minimize this type of failure, but in the long run it is not as serious as spiritual failure.[1]

1. Erwin Lutzer, *Failure: The Back Door to Success* (Chicago: Moody, 1975), pp. 41-42.

Lutzer devotes his entire book to failure in the Christian life, the first kind of failure, because he thinks that kind of failure has more serious consequences than the second type of failure. In one sense, that is true: one is morally guilty for failure due to sin. Failure in the Christian life breaks one's fellowship with God and has eternal consequences. We need to confess this type of failure to God, or we shall be held accountable and judged for it. So in the ultimate sense, the consequences of failure in the Christian life are far more serious than the ordinary failures that happen to occur in our lives.

On the other hand, however, in terms of everyday consequences in the world in which we live, it is not always true that the first type of failure has the more serious consequences. For if we do not know how to respond properly to it, failure in the life of a Christian can be even more devastating than failure that comes about specifically because of our sin.

Now I have no particular difficulty in understanding failure in the Christian life. Of course, sin leads to failure! What else could we expect? Nor is the solution to this sort of failure difficult to understand: repentance, confession, faith, and obedience. So I do not find failure in the Christian life puzzling, especially when I reflect on the weakness of my own flesh. It is not surprising that we sin and fail.

But the second type of failure is problematic to me. When someone is walking in faith and obedience to the Lord, how can he be led into the pit of failure? Think about it. How can obeying God's will lead to failure? This is, indeed, puzzling. Therefore, I want to focus our attention on this second kind of failure, failure in the life of a Christian, and to see if we can come to understand it.

For many years I had the point of view that Christians who are walking in God's will basically cannot fail. Perhaps I was just outrageously naive, but I don't think so. I had given the matter serious thought and had even qualified my position at several important points. For example, I distinguished failure from persecution. Scripture is clear that persons who are trying to live godly lives in Christ Jesus will experience persecution, and Jesus said that they will be blessed for it. Christians who have died in concentration camps because of their faith, or who have lost jobs or been discriminated against because they were Christians, could not properly be said to have failed.

I also distinguished failure from trials. The Scripture is clear that as Christians we are not exempt from trials and that such testing produces maturity and endurance. Without trials we would remain pampered and spoiled children. But I believed that if we endured our trials in reliance upon God's strength, He would see us through and bring us victoriously to the other side. Basically, it just did not make sense to me to say that God would call a person to do something and then—when that person was obedient to the call and was relying on God's strength—allow him to fail.

And, in fact, there is some Scripture support for the position I took. Look at what Psalm 1:1-3 says:

> Blessed is the man
>   who does not walk in the counsel of the wicked
> or stand in the way of sinners
>   or sit in the seat of mockers.
> But his delight is in the law of the Lord,
>   and on his law he meditates day and night.
> He is like a tree planted by streams of water,
>   which yields its fruit in season
> and whose leaf does not wither.
>   Whatsoever he does prospers.

What could be clearer? In all that he does, he prospers!

But then I experienced a disastrous personal failure that forced me to rethink this entire issue. It occurred while Jan and I were living in West Germany and I was finishing my doctoral studies in theology at the University of Munich under the famous theologian Wolfhart Pannenberg. My dissertation had already been approved, and all that remained was to pass the oral examination in theology (ominously called the *Rigorosum*). Not knowing what to expect I tried repeatedly to get an appointment with Pannenberg to discuss the examination and how I might prepare for it. But I was never able to succeed in seeing him (German professors tend to be much more reclusive than their American counterparts). So I went to his teaching assistant, a brilliant young theologian who had earned his doctorate under Pannenberg. He brushed aside the idea of preparing for the examination. "Forget it!" he advised. Well, I wasn't that stupid, so I pressed him further on how I might prepare. "Pannenberg always asks questions only over his own writings," he responded. "Just read what he has written."

That seemed to me to be a good strategy, and so over the next several weeks I read and studied virtually everything Pannenberg had ever written. I felt confident that I had mastered his thought.

On the day of the examination I entered Pannenberg's office. He would deliver the exam himself, and the process was to be monitored and recorded by the dean of the theology faculty and one other professor of theology. We shook hands all around and sat down for the questioning to commence.

Almost immediately things began to go wrong. Pannenberg began to ask questions on subjects that were not discussed in his writings. He began to ask about the particularities of this or that man's theology. *And I could not answer the questions.* Again and again I had to confess my ignorance. I cannot convey to you the feeling of helplessness and fear that swept over me. Question after question, I realized that I was watching my doctorate slip away before me, and—like trying to grasp sand slipping through your fingers—there was nothing I could do to stop it. This torture went on for nearly an hour. Near the end of the hour's examination, just to make my failure patently evident to all, Pannenberg asked a couple of condescendingly easy questions, as if to come down to my level of knowledge. My humiliation was complete.

Devastated, I left the theology department to meet Jan to go out to dinner at a restaurant where the two of us had planned to celebrate. She came rushing up to me, smiling, with a look of expectancy in her eyes. "Honey—I failed," I said. She couldn't believe it. We went out to dinner anyway, but it was an evening of sadness. It was just before Christmas, and on the twenty-third we had planned to fly back to the United States to visit my family and begin teaching at Trinity Evangelical Divinity School in Deerfield, Illinois, after the New Year. Now we were going home in defeat. As if to add injury to insult, on the flight back, Lufthansa lost our IBM typewriter, Jan's handbag where she had packed her most valuable personal effects was stolen, and I lost both my contact lenses!

But those material losses were nothing compared to the turmoil I felt inside over losing my doctorate. I just couldn't understand how God could have let it happen. He had called us to Germany and miraculously supplied the finances for my study. We were walking in His will; I was sure of it. I had not been negligent or overconfident. I had tried often to see Pannenberg in advance, but he was always too busy for me, so I prepared the best way I knew how. But especially, we had prayed earnestly and faithfully for this examination, and there were others, Spirit-filled Christians in the United States, praying for it, too. The examination had been entirely fair, I couldn't deny that. I had just failed it, that's all. But how could God have let it happen? What about His promises? "In all that he does, he prospers." "Whatsoever you ask in my name . . ."

It wasn't just that I had failed an examination. More than that, my failure was a spiritual crisis in faith for me. I felt hurt and disgraced, but even more, I felt betrayed by God. How could I ever trust Him again?

As I worked through my feelings in the ensuing days, it became clear to me that Psalm 1:1-3 just could not be construed as some sort of blanket promise that covers every case. Christians don't always prosper in what they undertake. Sometimes they do fail, and that's just a fact.

Now someone might again say, "You can't use human experience to nullify God's Word! His promises stand regardless of your experience." But the problem with this response is that Scripture itself gives examples of such failure. For instance, God had promised to give the land of Canaan to the twelve tribes of Israel. But in Judges 1:19, we read, "The Lord was with the men of Judah. They took possession of the hill country, but they were unable to drive the people from the plains, because they had iron chariots." Look at what it says here: *the Lord was with the armies of Judah*—but despite that fact, although they conquered the hill country, they failed to defeat their enemy in the plains because they had iron chariots! It doesn't seem to make sense: God was with them, and yet they failed. How are we to understand such failure in the life of the believer?

Now some people might answer that question by claiming that God has no specific will for our lives. God's will is His general desire that we obey His ethical and spiritual commands, that we arrive at a Christlike character, and so forth. But He has no specific will for individual persons that includes such matters as getting a doctorate, marrying a certain person, or entering into a particular business deal. So when we undertake those things, we do so wholly on our own initiative and may well wind up in failure.

But this solution strikes me as inadequate, despite its apparent appeal to many people. In the first place, it implies a deficient concept of God's sovereignty, providence, and guidance. Although the Bible teaches human freedom, it also has a strong emphasis on God's sovereign control and providential direction over everything that happens. Nothing happens in the world without God's directly willing it, or, in the case of sinful acts, at least permitting it. Moreover, God has so providentially ordered the world that His ends will be accomplished by the things we decide to undertake. Our decisions, then, cannot be a matter of indifference to Him. Moreover, He has promised to guide us in what we decide. All this suggests that God does have a specific will for our lives.

But that point aside, in the second place, this proposed solution doesn't actually get to the heart of the problem. For even if God does not have a specific will for our lives, the fact remains that He has promised to be with us, empowering and helping us. That is why the example in Judges is so puzzling. The Lord was with them, but still they failed. So even if God has no specific will for our lives, that still doesn't explain how we can fail in things we decide to do in His strength.

And so I was led to what was, for me, a radical new insight into the will of God, namely, that *God's will for our lives can include failure*. In other words, God's will may be that you fail, and He may lead you into failure! For there are things that God has to teach you through failure that He could never teach you through success.

In my own case, failing my doctoral exams forced me to see my life's priorities in a new light. When we returned to my folks for Christmas, I broke the news to my parents that I had failed my oral examination and didn't receive the doctorate. To my astonishment, my mother retorted, "Who cares?" I was stunned! To me it seemed like the catastrophe of a lifetime, but she just shrugged it off as though it didn't matter. It dawned on me that in one sense it really didn't, that there are things in life a good deal more important than doctorates, publications, and academic fame. In the end, it was human relationships that really mattered—especially family relationships.

My mind went back to a scientist we had met in Germany who had been divorced for many years and who wanted with all his heart to return to his wife and little boy. "When I was first married," he had told us, "I spent all my time in the laboratory. All I could think of was my research to the exclusion of anything or anyone else." It had seemed so important to him then. But now he knew it wasn't. "I was a fool," he said. And so I, too, now realized afresh the blessings I had in a faithful wife who had sacrificed and worked with me all those years I was in school and in loving parents who accepted me unconditionally just because I was their son. That Christmas marked the beginning of a new relationship with my folks. Jan and I have come to know them not merely as parents but as friends.

You see, I had failed to understand what true success

really is. True success is not achieving wealth, power, or fame. True success lies in the realm of the spiritual, or to be more specific, lies in getting to know God better. J. I. Packer expresses this thought succinctly in *Knowing God*:

> We have been brought to the point where we both can and must get our life's priorities straight. From current Christian publications you might think that the most vital issue for any real or would-be Christian in the world today is church union, or social witness, or dialogue with other Christians and other faiths, or refuting this or that -ism, or developing a Christian philosophy and culture, or what have you. But our line of study makes the present-day concentration on these things look like a gigantic conspiracy of misdirection. Of course, it is not that; the issues themselves are real and must be dealt with in their place. But it is tragic that, in paying attention to them, so many in our day seem to have been distracted from what was, is, and always will be the true priority for every human being—that is, learning to know God in Christ.[2]

When I first read this statement, it stunned me: "refuting this or that -ism or developing a Christian philosophy." Exactly the sort of thing I am about in life. And yet it is not the most important. One could succeed in it and yet, in God's sight, still be a failure.

That brings to mind a thought that came to haunt Lutzer as a busy pastor: "You may not be accomplishing as much as you think you are." We can be doing many things for the Lord and still fail to be the kind of person God desires us to be. Indeed, my greatest fear is that I should some day stand before the Lord and see all my works go up in smoke like so much "wood, hay, and stubble." What, after all, did Jesus say?—"The first shall be last, and the last shall be first." It is not success in the eyes of the world that ultimately counts, but success in the Lord's eyes.

Now this is both encouraging and convicting. On the one hand, it is encouraging because even though we fail,

2. J. I. Packer, *Knowing God* (London: Hodder & Stoughton, 1973), p. 314.

failure may be the better part of success in the Lord's eyes. I have a hunch that God is not so much interested in what we go through as in how we go through it. Though we may fail in the task that we've set out to do, if we respond to that failure with faith, courage, and dependency on the Lord's strength, rather than with despair, bitterness, and depression, we are counted a success in His sight.

On the other hand, it is convicting because we may think that we are accomplishing a lot when actually we are failing in the Lord's sight. The apostle Paul recognized that he could be a brilliant and gifted theologian, one who lived in poverty because of his generosity and who was even martyred for preaching the gospel, and yet, if he lacked love, be nothing in God's sight. For true success is found in loving God and your fellow man.

Well, what practical application does all this have for our lives? Two points can be made.

First, we need to learn from our failures. When we fail, we shouldn't adopt the sour grapes attitude of the fox in Aesop's fable. Instead, we should analyze our failure to see what lesson we can learn from it. That doesn't mean trying to figure out why God allowed it to happen. In many cases, we'll never know why. Too many Christians fall into what Packer calls the "York signal box mistake."[3] In the train yards in the city of York is a master control room containing an electronic panel showing in lights the position of every train in the yard. Someone in the control tower, who sees the whole panel, can understand just why a particular train was put on hold at one spot or why another was shunted into a siding somewhere else, even though to someone down on the tracks the movements of the trains may appear to be inexplicable. The Christian who wants to know why God permits every failure in his life is asking, Packer says, to be in God's "signal box," and yet, for better or for worse, we just don't have access to it. Therefore, it is pointless to torture ourselves about why God permitted this or that disaster to come into our lives.

3. Ibid, pp. 110-11.

But although we don't always discern or comprehend God's providential design, we can still learn from our failures. As Lutzer says, "It isn't necessary to know why God sent us the misfortune in order to profit from it."[4] Ask yourself what you should have done differently in your situation or what you could do differently next time. Ask yourself what sort of reaction God wants you to have, or what character trait can be developed in you as a result of the defeat. Learn from your failure.

Second, never give up. Just because you have failed, it's not all over for you. Here the example of a man like Richard Nixon is instructive. Narrowly defeated in the 1960 presidential election by John Kennedy, Nixon returned to his home state of California only to fail again in his bid for the governorship. It looked like his political career was over. "You won't have Dick Nixon to kick around anymore," he grumped to the press. But quietly he was laying the groundwork for a comeback. In 1968 he beat Hubert Humphrey for the presidency and in 1972 crushed his challenger George McGovern. Then came Watergate. Disgraced and facing impeachment, he ignominiously resigned the office of President. No one, I dare say, ever expected to hear much from him again.

But a few years later, there he was speaking at the Oxford University Debating Union and arguing on issues of public policy. He continued to do so, and a few years later *Newsweek* magazine ran a cover story on Nixon. On the front of the magazine, beside his picture, was the simple statement in large yellow letters "He's Back!" It summed up the fact that Nixon had come to be regarded as something of an elder statesman whose foreign policy opinions and shrewd political advice were much sought after.

When Nixon was asked at Oxford to explain the secret of his surprising comeback, he gave this advice, which we would do well to take to heart: "You're never through when you fail. You're only through when you quit. Never quit. Never, never, never."

4. Lutzer, p. 66.

That's good advice. You're not finished just because you fail. You're only finished if you give up and quit. But don't quit! With God's strength, pick up the pieces of your failure and, having learned from it, go on.

That's what we did in our case, and I'm glad to say that the story has a happy ending. At German universities, if you fail the oral examinations the first time, you can retake them. Jan and I both knew that I had to try again, and our friends encouraged us to do so. So after beginning to teach at Trinity Seminary, I spent the next entire year preparing again for the *Rigorosum*. I worked through Harnack's prodigious, three-volume *Dogmengeschichte*, Pelikan's multi-volume history of the Development of Doctrine, Cunliffe-Jones's *History of Christian Doctrine*, Loof's *Dogmengeschichte*, two lengthy study guides on the whole of Dogmatics prepared for German university students in theology, as well as studying the documents of the various councils and creeds of the church, readings in the church Fathers, works on contemporary theology, and so forth. By the time the year was out, I had a stack of notes about a foot high, which I had virtually memorized, and was prepared to answer questions on any area of systematic theology—be it Christology, anthropology, soteriology, or whatever—from the early Apologists to the Middle Ages, through the Reformation, the Enlightenment, and the twentieth century. I was set. But I was scared to death.

When I walked into Pannenberg's office, everything looked pretty much the same as before. But this time, it was different. Pannenberg began with the doctrine of the Trinity, starting with the *logos* doctrine of the early Apologists. And to my joy (which I could scarcely conceal!), as the examination continued to unfold I found myself readily responding to each question with full and accurate answers. The only question I tripped up on was one about why Hegel's doctrine of the incarnation entailed the death of God—and I didn't feel so bad about missing that one! Pannenberg himself was clearly delighted with my success and awarded me a *magna cum laude* for the examination. I was dancing on air!

So it was a victory for the Lord in the end. But the victory was not just in passing the examination. For, not to mention the spiritual lessons God taught me, I discovered a sobering truth. Like so many other American students, I had been woefully trained in seminary in the history of Christian doctrine. The training in systematic theology that American evangelical seminaries generally give their students is but a pale shadow of what German university students in theology receive. Is it therefore any wonder that sceptical German theology leads the world? How can we ever hope that evangelical theology will become a leading model unless we begin to train our students with the same rigor and thoroughness that characterize German theological instruction? I can say without hesitation that during that year of intense study I learned more about systematic theology than I did during my entire seminary training. So although I would never want to relive my experience, I can honestly say that I'm glad I failed the exam the first time around. It was for the best, because as a result of that failure I became theologically equipped for the Lord's service in a way that would never have been possible if I had passed.

And I'm so glad that we didn't quit. Suppose we had just given up. Let's say that in the humiliation of my failure, I had lost hope and not tried to take the exam the second time. The pangs of defeat would have haunted me every time I thought of my failure or opened a book on systematic theology. I would not have had that year of intensive study, and I would have remained in my anemic state of theological knowledge. The years would have passed, and I would have continually asked myself the question: *Should I have tried again?* Even if I had tried and failed the second time, I would still have been better off than by quitting. To paraphrase an old motto in a different context: It is better to have tried and failed than not to have tried at all.

So when you encounter failure, don't give up. Ask God for the strength to go on. He will give it to you. In fact, there is a biblical name for that quality. It is called *endurance*. Through failure, if you respond correctly, God can build the quality of endurance into your life.

Failure in the life of a Christian, then, should not surprise us. God has important things to teach us through failure—and true success, the success that counts for eternity, consists in learning those lessons. So when you fail, do not despair or think that God has abandoned you; rather, learn from your failures and never give up. That is the formula for success.

4
Suffering and Evil (I)

Undoubtedly the greatest intellectual obstacle to belief in God—for both the Christian and the non-Christian—is the so-called problem of evil. That is to say, it seems unbelievable that if an all-powerful and all-loving God exists, He would permit so much pain and suffering in the world.

The amount of human misery and pain in the world is, indeed, incalculable. On the one hand, there are all the evils that are the result of man's own inhumanity to man. One small, historical example can be cited from the reign of Emperor Basil II, who ruled the Byzantine Empire from the capital city of Constantinople from 975 to 1025. In 1003 the Bulgarian Czar Samuel conquered Macedonia, and four years later Basil II, who had earned the nickname "slayer of the Bulgarians" because of his frequent wars with that kingdom, took it back. There followed years of indecisive conflict until in 1014 Basil II annihilated the Bulgarian army at Balathista. Not content with victory, he proceeded to put out the eyes of several thousand Bulgarian soldiers who had survived the battle and sent this blind army back to Czar Samuel, who, overwhelmed at the spectacle of his maimed and groping troops, died of shock. What a hideous, devastating spectacle that must have been!

Unlike the beasts, man seems to have a penchant for almost unimaginable cruelty to others. Perhaps the most forceful way to bring this home is to read a book such as Robert P. Mannix's *History of Torture* or to visit a medieval castle and look at the terrible devices used to inflict pain on prisoners. What is especially sickening is that historically the church has been part of this barbarism. Between 1096 and 1274, for example, the medieval church launched eight major Crusades, as well as numerous smaller ventures, aimed at liberating the Holy Land from Islamic control. These expeditions, which were characterized by greed, deceit, and the lust for power, accomplished almost nothing and resulted in the loss of thousands of lives. The fourth Crusade, for example, launched in 1204, was supposed to be aimed at Egypt, but at the last minute the Crusaders diverted the mission and sacked instead the Christian city of Zara and then attacked Constantinople, the capital of the eastern Christian empire, pillaging the city with what one historian described as "unparalleled horrors." But the most heinous of these expeditions was the so-called Children's Crusade of 1212. In this ludicrous mission, thousands of children were recruited to form an army to liberate the Holy Land. But the children never got any farther than Marseille, France. There they were kidnaped and sold into slavery by the leaders of the Crusade.

The history of mankind is a history of bloodshed and war. Sometime ago on the public television station I saw a ten-part serial, "The World at War," which presented a history of the Second World War. The last installment of the program calculated the lives lost in that conflict: 6 million Jews slain in Nazi concentration camps, 16 million lives lost in Germany, 20 million persons killed in the Soviet Union, and so on. The numbers were staggering. In all, some 51 million people were killed in World War II. Think of it! And that says nothing of the millions and millions of wounded, of the untold suffering of the living, of the poverty, starvation, dehumanization, immorality, and disruption of normal lives that war throws up in its wake. And lest those statistics numb us by their inconceivability, we ought to remind ourselves that each of those people died *one at a time.*

Perhaps no one has stated more powerfully than the great Russian novelist Fyodor Dostoyevsky the objection that human, moral evil poses to the existence of God. In a scene in the novel *The Brothers Karamazov* the atheist Ivan explains to his brother Alyosha, a Russian Orthodox priest, how evil in the world makes it impossible for him to believe in God:

"By the way, a Bulgarian I met lately in Moscow," Ivan went on, seeming not to hear his brother's words, "told me about the crimes committed by Turks and Circassians in all parts of Bulgaria through fear of a general rising of the Slavs. . . . People talk sometimes of bestial cruelty, but that's a great injustice and insult to the beast; a beast can never be so cruel as a man, so artistically cruel. . . . These Turks took a pleasure in torturing children, too; cutting the unborn child from the mother's womb, and tossing babies up in the air and catching them on the points of their bayonets before their mother's eyes. Doing it before the mother's eyes was what gave zest to the amusement. Here is another scene that I thought very interesting. Imagine a trembling mother with her baby in her arms, a circle of invading Turks around her. They've planned a diversion: they pet the baby, laugh to make it laugh. They succeed, the baby laughs. At that moment a Turk points a pistol four inches from the baby's face. The baby laughs with glee, holds out its little hands to the pistol, and he pulls the trigger in the baby's face and blows out its brains. Artistic, wasn't it. . . .

"But I've still better things about children. I've collected a great, great deal about Russian children, Alyosha. There was a little girl of five who was hated by her father and mother, most worthy and respectable people, of good education and breeding. . . . This poor child of five was subjected to every possible torture by those cultivated parents. They beat her, thrashed her, kicked her for no reason till her body was one bruise. Then, they went to greater refinements of cruelty—shut her up all night in the cold and frost in a privy, and because she didn't ask to be taken up at night (as though a child of five sleeping its angelic, sound sleep could be trained to wake and ask), they smeared her face and filled her mouth with excrement, and it was her mother, her mother did this. And that mother could sleep, hearing the poor child's groans! Can you understand why a little creature, who can't even understand what's done to her, should beat her little aching heart with her tiny fist in the dark and the cold, and weep her meek unresentful tears to dear, kind God to protect her? . . . Do you understand why this infamy must be and is permitted? Without it, I am told, man could not have existed on earth, for he could not have known good and evil. Why should he know that diabolical good and evil when it costs so much? Why, the whole world of knowledge is not worth that child's prayer to dear, kind God!"[1]

Such moral evil is bad enough, but perhaps even more difficult to reconcile with the existence of an all-powerful and loving God is the presence of evils brought on by natural causes in the world. One thinks of natural disasters, such as floods, earthquakes, or tornadoes; of the different sorts of diseases, such as smallpox, polio, cancer, or leukemia; of congenital disabilities, such as muscular distrophy, cerebral palsy, or enecephalitis; of accidents and injuries, such as being burned, drowning, or falling. Sometimes these natural evils are intertwined with human evils: for example, there are countries in which millions face starvation, not because there are not enough relief supplies to meet the need, but because the government will not permit those supplies to reach the people but instead uses food as a political weapon to crush rebel resistance.

A few years ago the horror of natural evils was graphically displayed in two incidents shown on television. In Mexico City a terrible earthquake had devastated blocks of high rise apartment buildings. As rescue teams in the aftermath of the quake searched the rubble for survivors, they came across a ten year old boy who was trapped alive somewhere in the recesses of a collapsed building. During the next several days, the whole world watched in agony as the teams tried to remove the rubble to get to the boy. They could communicate with him, but could not reach him. His grandfather, who had been trapped with him, was already dead. "I'm scared!" he cried. After about eleven days, there

---

1. Fyodor Dostoyevsky, *The Brothers Karamazov*, trans. Constance Garnett (New York: New American Library, 1957), pp. 219-23.

was silence. Alone in the darkness, trapped without food and water, afraid, the little boy died before the rescue teams could free him.

That same year a mudslide swept over a village in Colombia. As rescuers came to help survivors, they came across a little girl who was pinned up to her chin in muddy water. For some reason or other, they could not free her or remove the water. All they could do was stand by helplessly and watch her die. Every night on the news we saw films of the little girl's decline. It was the most pathetic sight I have ever seen. She stood there, unable to move, spitting out the water that continually flowed into her mouth. As the days went by, she became more exhausted, and deep, black circles formed under her eyes. She was dying before our very eyes, as we watched on television. Finally, the evening newscaster reported that she was gone.

Those two incidents rent my heart. *Oh, God!* I thought. *How could You permit those children to die like that? If they had to die, so be it. But You could have let the boy be killed instantly by the collapse of the building or let the little girl drown suddenly. Why these tortuous, pointless, lingering deaths?* I'll be honest with you. When I see these sorts of things go on, it makes it hard to believe in God.

When I was a very young Christian, I thought that such things didn't happen to Christians who were walking in God's will. Didn't Romans 8:28 say that "we know that in all things God works for the good of those who love him, who have been called according to his purpose"? Christians who experienced pointless, gratuitous suffering must have strayed from God's will. But such a naive outlook is obviously incorrect, for the righteous and innocent *do* suffer. I think of a prominent Christian leader in my home town who was decapitated in a sledding accident when he ran into a barbed wire fence he hadn't seen; or of a pastor who backed out of his driveway and killed his infant son, who had been playing behind the car; or of some Canadian missionaries who were forced to return from the field when their little daughter fell from her third story window to the concrete driveway below and suffered severe brain damage. Clearly, Christians have not been exempted from the apparently pointless evils of the world.

In light of the quantity and nature of the suffering brought on by human or natural causes, how can it be that an all-powerful, all-good God exists? This is a question that must trouble many people, for a few years ago a Jewish author was able to make his book a best seller by titling it *Why Do Bad Things Happen to Good People?* Unfortunately, he could not solve the problem, for he could answer the question only by denying that God is all-powerful. But if we stick with the biblical conception of God, how are we to account for the existence of evil in a world that was made and is sustained by an all-powerful, all-good God?

Let me begin by making a number of distinctions to help us to keep our thinking straight. In the first place, we must distinguish between the intellectual problem of evil and the emotional problem of evil. The *intellectual* problem of evil concerns how to give a rational explanation of God and evil. The *emotional* problem of evil concerns how to comfort or console those who are suffering and how to dissolve the emotional dislike people have of a God who would permit such evil. The intellectual problem is in the province of the philosopher; the emotional problem is in the province of the counselor. It is important to understand this distinction, because the solution to the intellectual problem is apt to appear dry, uncaring, and uncomforting to someone who is going through suffering, whereas the solution to the emotional problem is apt to appear deficient as an explanation of evil to someone contemplating it abstractly.

Keeping this distinction in mind, let us turn first to the intellectual problem of evil.

Here again, we need to make another distinction. There are two versions of the intellectual problem of evil, the *logical* problem and the *probabilistic* problem. In the logical version of the problem, the atheist's goal is to show that it is logically impossible for both God and evil to exist, just as it is logically inconsistent to say that an irresistible force and an immovable object both exist. The two are logically incompatible. If one exists, the other does not. Yet since we know evil exists, the argument goes, it follows logically that God must not exist. In the probabilistic version of the problem of evil, the admission is made that if it is possible that God and evil both exist, it is pretty unlikely that He would permit evil. But since evil does exist, it seems improbable that God exists.

Let's examine each of these versions of the argument in turn.

First, *the logical problem of evil*. As we have noted, this version of the problem holds that the two statements "An all-powerful, all-good God exists" and "Evil exists" are logically inconsistent. They cannot both be true.

Now at face value, those statements are not inconsistent. There is not an explicit contradiction between them. So the objector must have in mind some hidden assumptions that make it logically inconsistent that there should be both God and evil. But what are those assumptions?

There seem to be two: (1) if God is all-powerful, then He can create any world that He chooses, and (2) since God is all-good, then He would prefer a world without evil over a world with evil. The objector reasons that since God is all-powerful, He could create a world containing free creatures who always freely choose to do right. Such a world would be a sinless world, free of all human, moral evils. By the same token, being all-powerful, God could as well create a world in which no natural evils ever occurred. It would be a world free of evil, pain, and suffering.

Now notice that the objector is *not* saying that men would be mere puppets in such a world. No, he's saying that it's *possible* for a world to exist in which everyone freely makes the right decision. Such a world *must* be possible, for it were not, we would be saying that sin is necessary, which would be unbiblical. Thus whenever a moral decision is made, it is theoretically possible to decide to do the right thing. So we can imagine a world in which everyone freely chose every time to do the right things, and, since God is all-powerful, He must be able to create it.

But since God is also all-good, the objector continues, He would, of course, prefer such a world to any world infected with evil. If God had the choice between creating a flawless world and a world with evil in it like this one, He would surely choose the flawless world. Otherwise, He would Himself be evil to prefer that His creatures experience pain and suffering when He could have given them happiness and prosperity.

The eighteenth-century Scottish skeptic David Hume summarized the logical problem of evil nicely when he asked concerning God, "Is He willing to prevent evil, but not able? Then He is impotent. Is He able, but not willing? Then He is malevolent. Is He both able and willing? Whence then is evil?"[2]

But the fallacy with this line of argument is that the two assumptions made by the objector are not necessarily true. In the first place, it is not necessarily true that an all-powerful God can create just any possible world. God's being all-powerful does not mean that He can do logical impossibilities, such as make a round square, or *make* someone *freely* choose to do something. For if you cause a person to make a specific choice, then the choice is no longer free. Thus, if God grants people genuine freedom to choose as they like, then it is impossible for Him to guarantee what their choices will be. All He can do is create the circumstances in which a person is able to make a free choice and then stand back and let him make that choice. Now what that means is that there may be worlds which are possible in and of themselves, but which God is incapable of creating. Suppose, for example, that in every world where God created free creatures those creatures would freely choose to do evil. In such a case, it is the creatures themselves who bring about the evil, and God can do nothing to prevent their doing so unless He removes their free will. Thus it is possible that every world God could create containing free creatures would be a world with sin and evil.

Moreover, as for natural evils, those could be the re-

2. David Hume, *Dialogues Concerning Natural Religion*, edited with an introduction by Norman Kemp Smith (Indianapolis: Bobbs-Merrill, 1980), part 10, p. 198.

sult of demonic activity in the world. Demons have free-dom just as do human beings, and it is possible that God could not preclude natural evil without removing the free will of demonic creatures. Now you might be thinking that such a resolution to the problem of natural evil is ridicu-lous and even frivolous, but then you would be confusing the *logical* problem of evil with the *probabilistic* problem of evil. Admittedly, ascribing all evil to demonic beings is im-probable, but that is strictly irrelevant here. All we are trying to show now is that such an explanation is possible and that, as a consequence, the objector's argument that God and evil are logically incompatible fails.

So the first assumption made by the objector, namely, that an all-powerful God can create any world that He chooses, is just not necessarily true. Therefore, the objec-tor's argument on this ground alone is invalid.

But what about the second assumption, that if God is all-good, then He would prefer a world without evil over a world with evil? Again, such an assumption is not necessar-ily true. The fact is that in many cases we allow pain and suffering to occur in a person's life in order to bring about some greater good or because we have some sufficient rea-son for allowing it. Every parent knows this fact. There comes a point at which a parent can no longer protect his child from every scrape, bruise, or mishap; and there are other times when discipline must be inflicted on the child in order to teach him to become a mature, responsible, adult. Similarly, God may permit suffering in our lives to build us or to test us, or to build and test others, or to achieve some other overriding end.

Sometimes this process can be very painful, as C. S. Lewis discovered upon the death of his wife. Comparing God to a Cosmic Surgeon rather than to a Cosmic Sadist, Lewis mused,

> The terrible thing is that a perfectly good God is . . . hardly less formidable than a Cosmic Sadist. The more we believe that God hurts only to heal, the less we can believe that there is any use in begging for tenderness. A cruel man

might be bribed—might grow tired of his vile sport—might have a temporary fit of mercy, as alcoholics have fits of sobriety. But suppose that what you are up against is a surgeon whose intentions are wholly good. The kinder and more conscientious he is, the more inexorably he will go on cutting. If he yielded to your entreaties, if he stopped before the operation was complete, all the pain up to that point would have been useless.

What do people mean when they say, "I am not afraid of God because I know He is good"? Have they never even been to a dentist?[3]

Thus, even though God is all-good, He might well have sufficient reason for permitting pain and suffering in the world. Consequently, the second assumption of our objector, that an all-good God would prefer a world with no evil over a world with evil, is not necessarily true.

The bottom line is that the logical version of the problem of evil does not stand up to scrutiny. No one has been able to formulate a valid argument to prove that God and evil are inconsistent.

But those who propound the logical problem of evil can regroup and return for a second wave of attack. They can admit that there is no inconsistency between God and evil in general but still argue that the existence of God is inconsistent with the *quantity* and *quality* of evil in the world. In other words, though abstractly speaking there is no inconsistency between God and evil, there is an inconsistency between God and the amount and kinds of evil that actually exist. For example, even if God's existence is compatible with, say, the fact that innocent persons are sometimes murdered, it is not compatible with the fact that so *many* people are killed and that they are killed in such tortuous, gruesome ways. An all-good and powerful God would not permit such things to happen.

But the crucial assumption behind this reasoning is the notion that God *cannot have morally sufficient reasons for permitting the amount and kinds of evil that exist.* The failing

3. C. S. Lewis, *A Grief Observed* (London: Faber & Faber, 1985), pp. 55-56.

in the assumption is that it is just not clear that the assumption is *necessarily* true. Consider first the amount of evil in the world. As terrible a place as the world is, there is still on balance a great deal more good in the world than evil. Otherwise everyone would commit suicide. But people generally agree that despite its ills life is worth living, and when things are going bad, people characteristically look to the future in the hope that things will get better.

Now it is possible, given human freedom, that in any other world God could have created, the balance between good and evil would have been even worse than in this one. That is to say, any world containing less *evil* might also have contained less *good*. Maybe the world we presently have has in it the most good God could get for the least amount of evil. Now you might say that seems pretty unlikely. But then you would be confusing once again the *logical* problem of evil with the *probabilistic* problem of evil. To refute the logical version of the problem of evil, the Christian does not have to suggest a *plausible* or *likely* solution—all he has to do is suggest a *possible* one. All he needs to do is show God and the amount of evil in the world are both *possible*, and that he seems to have done.

Now consider the *kinds* of evil in the world. The Christian believes that God has overriding reasons for permitting the world's most terrible atrocities to occur. For example, it may be that God places such a premium on human freedom that He is willing to permit atrocities to occur rather than to remove the free will of those who commit them. (Perhaps God will punish the wrong-doers in the afterlife and comfort those who were victimized, but that is beside the point at this stage of the argument.) Similarly, if we adopt the hypothesis that natural evils are the result of the free activity of demons, then the same point about free will applies there, too. Now it still might be objected that God could have created a world of free creatures in which they committed fewer atrocities. But then the same argument applies as before: though it is possible that in such a world there would be less *evil*, there might also have been less *good*.

The point is, if the objector aims to show that it is logically impossible for God and the evil in the world to both exist, then he has to prove that God cannot have morally sufficient reasons for permitting the amount and kinds of evil that exist. And he hasn't given us any proof for that assumption.

We can go even further than this. Not only has the objector failed to prove that God and evil are inconsistent, but we can, on the contrary, prove that they are consistent. In order to do that, all we have to do is provide some possible explanation of the evil in the world that is compatible with God's existence. And the following is such an explanation:

God could not have created a world that had so much good as the actual world but had less evil, both in terms of quantity and quality; and, moreover, God has morally sufficient reasons for the evil that exists.

So long as this explanation is even possible, it proves that God and the evil in the world are logically compatible.

So, to sum up our discussion of the logical problem of evil, we have seen that there is no necessary incompatibility between the presence of an all-good, all-powerful God and the presence of evil in the world. And I'm extremely pleased to report to you that after centuries of discussion, contemporary philosophy has come to recognize this fact. It is now widely admitted that the logical problem of evil has been solved. (Praise the Lord for Christian philosophers like Alvin Plantinga to whom this result is due!)[4]

But before we breathe too easily, we have to confront the probabilistic problem of evil. This we shall do in the next chapter.

---

4. This chapter is a popularization of the Free Will Defense laid out by Plantinga in *The Nature of Necessity* (Oxford: Clarendon Press, 1974), pp. 164-95; see further, Alvin Plantinga, "Self-Profile" in James Tomberlin and Peter Van Inwagen, eds., *Alvin Plantinga*, Profiles, no. 5. (Dordrecht, Holland: D. Reidel, 1985), pp. 36-55.

5
Suffering and Evil (II)

When we consider the probabilistic problem of evil, things are not so easy. For even though the explanation of evil I gave in the last chapter is possible, still it seems wildly improbable. Explaining all natural evil as the result of demons, for example, seems ridiculous. Does anyone really believe that earthquakes are the result of demons moving tectonic plates about or that when he stubs his toe the devil made him do it? And couldn't God reduce the evil in the world without reducing the good? To recall the tragedy in Mexico City, what impairment of the good of the world would have resulted if the child had simply died in the collapse of the building instead of lingering eleven days in agony? The world is filled with so many seemingly pointless and unnecessary evils that it seems doubtful that God could have any sort of morally sufficient reason for permitting them. Accordingly, it might be argued that given the evil in the world, it is improbable, even if not impossible, that God exists.

Now this is a much more powerful argument than the purely logical problem of evil. Since its conclusion is more modest ("It is improbable that God exists"), it is much easier to prove. What shall we say about this argument? Is it improbable that God exists?

Well, to begin with, let's note a very important—indeed, crucial—difference between a probability argument like this one and a purely logical argument like the one we had before. In the case of a purely logical argument, all you

have to consider is the argument itself. If the logical problem of evil is a sound argument, then God cannot exist,
period, no questions asked. But with a probability argument, we have to ask, probable with respect to what? To
give an illustration: suppose Joe is a college student. Suppose, further, that 95 percent of college students drink beer.
With respect to that information, it makes it highly probable that Joe drinks beer. But suppose we find out that Joe
is a Wheaton College student and that 95 percent of Wheaton students do not drink beer. Suddenly the probability of
Joe's being a beer drinker has changed dramatically! The
point is that probabilities are relative to what background
information is considered.

Now apply this principle to the probabilistic problem
of evil. It claims to prove that God's existence is improbable. But with respect to what? To the evil in the world? If
that's all you consider, then I would hardly be surprised
that God's existence should appear improbable. Indeed, I
would consider it to be a major philosophical achievement
if Christians could demonstrate that relative to the evil in
the world alone, God's existence is not improbable. But the
Christian needn't be committed to such an arduous task.
He will insist that we consider, not just the evil in the
world, but all the evidence relevant to God's existence,
including the ontological argument for a maximally great
being, the cosmological argument for a Creator of the universe, the teleological argument for an intelligent Designer
of the cosmos, the personalistic argument for an ultimate
Mind, the moral argument for an ultimate, personally-embodied Good, as well as evidence concerning the person of
Christ, the historicity of the resurrection, the existence of
miracles, plus existential and religious experience. When
we take into account the full scope of the evidence, the
existence of God becomes very probable. Hence, a Christian could actually admit that the problem of evil, taken in
isolation, does make God's existence improbable. But he
will insist that when the total scope of the evidence is
considered, then the scales are at least even or tip in favor
of Christianity. Indeed, if he includes the self-authenticat-

ing witness of the Holy Spirit as part of his total evidence, then he can rightly assert that he knows that God exists, even if he has no solution at all to the problem of evil.

So even though the probabilistic problem of evil is a lot easier to prove than the logical problem of evil, it is, even when successful, a whole lot less decisive.

But is it in fact successful? This is far from clear. For one thing the notion of probability is far from clear. It tends to have a heavily subjective element to it. In ambiguous cases, what may appear improbable to one person may not seem improbable at all to somebody else. The problem of evil seems to be like this. Given the existence of the evil in the world, is it improbable that God exists? Well, that depends on how probable it is that God has morally sufficient reasons for permitting the evil that occurs.

What makes the probability here so difficult to assess is that we are just so ignorant of God's designs. We are simply not in a position to know why God permits certain evils to occur. Certainly many evil events seem pointless and gratuitous to us—but how can we be sure they really are? Perhaps they fit into a wider picture. According to the biblical scheme of things, God is directing human history toward His previsioned ends. Now can you possibly imagine the complexity of planning and directing a world of free creatures toward some end without violating their freedom? Think of the innumerable, incalculable contingencies involved in arriving at a single historical event, say, the Allied victory at D-day! It may well be that in order to arrive at some end, God must permit sinful actions and natural evils to enter into the picture.

Take the Holocaust, for example. Few more horrific events in history can be imagined. Probably millions of people lost their faith in God through this cataclysm. But suppose that the only way God could get the nations of the world to freely establish the modern state of Israel was by allowing the Holocaust, an event so ghastly, so unparalleled in history, directed at a single persecuted people, that the world in shame and sympathy took the remarkable step of restoring the Jews to their ancient homeland. I want to say emphatically that this does not mean the Holocaust was, after all, good. That would be absurd. It was a hideous illustration of human depravity, sin piled upon sin, contrary to God's perfect will. But perhaps God had a morally sufficient reason to permit it, namely, the establishment of the nation of Israel. A church Father once said of the early Christian martyrs that the blood of the martyrs was the seed of the church. Perhaps future generations of Israelis will say with gratitude the same thing of those who died in the Holocaust. And who knows what future plans God has in store for the nation of Israel? Perhaps Israel will play so significant a role in world events that all nations will see that God had a morally sufficient reason for permitting the Holocaust.

The same point might be made on an individual level. We just don't know how the sufferings we endure might be used of God in our lives or, if not in ours, in the lives of those around us. Yes, they often look pointless, but we are simply not in a position to judge.

The point I'm trying to make is that assessments of probability with regard to evil can be very difficult and subjective. It is far from obvious that the evil in the world makes it improbable that God exists.

But much more can be said concerning the probabilistic problem of evil. The atheist maintains that if God exists, then it is improbable that the world would contain the evil it does. Now what the Christian can do in response to such an assertion is to offer various hypotheses that would tend to raise the probability of evil given God's existence. The Christian can show that if God exists and these hypotheses are true, then it is not so surprising that evil exists. Therefore, the existence of this evil doesn't render God's existence improbable.[1]

What are some of those hypotheses? They are doc-

---

1. I am indebted for the following to Robert Merrihew Adams, "Plantinga on the Problem of Evil," in *Alvin Plantinga*, pp. 225-55; and to Marilyn McCord Adams, "Problem of Evil: More Advice to Christian Philosophers," *Faith and Philosophy* 5 (1988):121-43.

trines that emerge from the Christian concept of God. It turns out that answering the probabilistic problem of evil is easier from the Christian perspective than from the perspective of belief in the mere existence of God.

To begin with, according to the biblical view, what is the purpose of life and the end of man? To know God. In John 17:3 Jesus said, "Now this is eternal life: that they may know you, the only true God, and Jesus Christ, whom you have sent." But mankind is in rebellion against God's purpose and finds itself alienated from God, morally guilty before Him, and groping in spiritual darkness. The terrible human evils I described at the beginning of this chapter are testimony to man's depravity. The Christian is not surprised at the human evil in the world; on the contrary, he expects it. The Scriptures indicate that God gave man up to the sin he had freely chosen; He does not interfere to stop it but lets human depravity run its course. In addition to human evil, there is a realm of beings higher than man also in rebellion against God, demonic creatures, incredibly evil, in whose power the creation lies and who seek to destroy God's work and thwart His purposes. God sets limits on their destructive work and by His Spirit seeks to draw men from under their power into His kingdom.

He gave His moral law to Israel that the heinousness of sin might become especially evident, in order that men might repent, turn to Him for forgiveness, and be saved. Finally, He sent His Son to die as an expiatory sacrifice to bear mankind's guilt and punishment for sin, that through Him men could come into a personal relationship with God. Those who come to know Him through His Son Jesus are adopted into God's family, are quickened and strengthened by His Spirit, and though not snatched out of this evil world or exempted from its suffering, are given grace to endure until God takes them home. In the life to come, the heavenly Father will bestow upon His children unspeakable joy and blessing and reward them for their faithfulness, whereas those who continued in sin and spurned God will receive their just punishment.

Some of the elements of this story were already components of our defense against the logical problem of evil. It is plausible, for example, that creaturely free will is the source of moral evil in the world. Moreover, it is plausible that God could not have created a world of free creatures without evil's being involved. It is plausible that any world with this much moral good would also entail a great deal of evil wrought by sin. As for natural evil, it is plausible that some is due to demonic activity. Finally, some naturally caused pain and suffering may be justified in light of the higher goods they yield.

But these elements of the story don't answer all our questions. Let's look at moral evil first. The problem here concerns the amount and kinds of evil in the world. It seems plausible that the world could have had just as much good as it has, but with less evil. Much of the pain and suffering we observe seems absolutely pointless and unnecessary. For example, would the world have been any worse if God had intervened to prevent the Children's Crusade? All that might appear to be sacrificed would be the cherished free will of the villains who kidnapped them—and is it really all so important to the world's overall goodness to preserve that?

But this is where our Christian hypotheses enter in. One reason the problem of evil seems so devastating is that we tend to think that God's purpose in the world is to achieve human happiness in this life. But in the Christian view that is false. God's purpose for man is not happiness but holiness. Man's end is the knowledge of God. Moreover, that purpose is not restricted to this life but spills over into eternity beyond the grave. Finally, knowledge of God is what philosophers call an incommensurable good, that is to say, it is a good so great that it is immeasurable and incomparable. The privilege of personally knowing the infinite God, the Creator of the universe and the source of all goodness, infinitely outstrips anything else in all the world.

When we grasp this, it becomes evident that many evils that seem pointless or unnecessary with regard to producing human happiness may not after all be such with regard to producing knowledge of God. Dostoyevsky, who stated the problem of evil so forcefully, saw this point and sought to answer the problem in his novels through the portrayal of characters who through suffering increase in godliness and holiness. The apostle Paul prayed to the Lord that he might know Him and share His sufferings (Philippians 3:10). Jesus Himself was said to be perfected through suffering (Hebrews 2:10). It might be objected that people also turn against God because of their sufferings. That is certainly true. But notice then that it is a matter of our free choice. God's desire is that all men come to know Him through Jesus Christ and be filled with His Spirit. Innocent human suffering provides an occasion for deeper dependency and faith in God. It all depends on how we respond. Hence, some evil may serve no earthly good whatsoever, but for its victims it is a summons to a deeper knowledge of God.

In some cases, evil may not lead to a deeper knowledge of God on the part of the victim, for example, when infants suffer. But in many such cases, their suffering may be the occasion for intense suffering on the part of those around them, for example, their parents. For these others, then, this evil presents an occasion upon which they must seek to draw closer to God for strength or comfort. We've probably all heard stories, for example, of how people have been brought to Christ and salvation by witnessing the suffering of others, particularly Christians.

Moreover, there is an eternal life following this one that awaits those who have trusted God in faith and obedience in this life. When God asks His children to bear horrible suffering in this life, it is with the prospect of a heavenly joy and recompense that is beyond all comprehension.

The apostle Paul, for example, underwent suffering for the sake of the gospel that was, when you reflect on it, unbelievable. It would be a devastating experience, not only physically excruciating but possibly even permanently crippling emotionally, to be whipped for a crime you didn't commit. But Paul was whipped five different times just for preaching the gospel, each time receiving twenty-six lashes to the back and thirteen to his breast with a triple-thonged whip. Not only that, but three times more he was stripped and beaten by Roman authorities with wooden rods. On one occasion in the city of Lystra he was surrounded by a mob, who stoned him and dragged his body out of the city, leaving him for dead. Can you imagine what it must feel like to be stoned? You could probably only pray that someone would knock you out quickly with a rock to the head; but probably you wouldn't be so lucky. It would be a horrible way to die. Paul's body must have been a mass of scars, wounds inflicted for no better reason than his being a Christian. No wonder he could say indignantly of those who denied his apostleship, "Finally, let no one cause me trouble, for I bear on my body the marks of Jesus" (Galatians 6:17).

People who have been imprisoned, even for a few months, have also testified what a life-shattering experience this sort of confinement can be. But Paul was frequently imprisoned for his faith for lengthy intervals in Roman jails, under what by modern standards could only be described as unspeakable conditions: unheated, unsanitary, bound hand and foot with chains. He called himself "a prisoner for Jesus Christ."

On top of all this, Paul suffered from natural disasters, too. For example, he apparently suffered from a debilitating illness, which some have speculated to have been epilepsy or some sort of eye disease. Furthermore, he was involved in three separate shipwrecks on the Mediterranean Sea. Can you imagine what it would be like to be involved in even one wreck at sea? But three times? And in one of those, Paul was adrift at sea for a night and a day before being saved. Can you imagine the terror of being adrift at sea in the night, desperately clutching some piece of wreckage, trying to fight off exhaustion, hour after hour, in constant peril of drowning? Moreover, in his travels throughout the Roman Empire preaching the gospel, Paul was constantly in danger from both human enemies and natural disasters. There were dangerous river crossings, and robbers were a threat while on the road. At any time, whether in the cities where he preached, or in the countryside, or at sea while he traveled, he could be set upon by enemies who sought his life. Whether those enemies were Jews, Gentiles, or false brethren, each of them had their particular reasons to get rid of Paul. He worked long, hard hours, often going without sleep, frequently without food, and without adequate protection from exposure to the elements. And psychologically, he bore the constant burden of anxiety for the fledgling Christian churches he had founded, which seemed to be in constant danger of being torn apart by heresies. In the end Paul made the ultimate sacrifice and was executed for his faith in Rome.

In sum, his life as an apostle was a life of incredible hardship and suffering, one which he described as punctuated by "afflictions, hardships, calamities, beatings, imprisonments, tumults, labors, watching, hunger" (2 Corinthians 6:4-5, RSV); the apostles were ignominious, misunderstood, and slandered, and possessed virtually nothing materially in this world. And yet Paul bore his sufferings without bitterness. Why? *Because it was worth it.* He understood that this life is but the cramped and narrow foyer that opens up into the great hall of eternal life, and he longed to go and be with Christ. He wrote,

> So we do not lose heart. Though our outer nature is wasting away, our inner nature is being renewed every day. For this slight momentary affliction is preparing for us an eternal weight of glory beyond all comparison, because we look not to the things that are seen but to the things that are unseen; for the things that are seen are transient, but the things that are unseen are eternal. (2 Corinthians 4:16-18; RSV)

Can you believe it? After what this man suffered, he calls it a "light and momentary" trouble! You see, Paul lived this life in the perspective of eternity. He imagined, as it were, a scale, in which all the sufferings and rottenness of this life were placed on the one side, while on the other side was placed the glory which God will give to His children in heaven. The weight of that glory was so great that it was literally beyond comparison with the sufferings. Similarly, the length of this life, being finite, is literally infinitesimal in comparison with the eternal life we shall spend with God. The longer we spend in eternity, the more the sufferings of this life will shrink toward a mere moment. That's why Paul called the sufferings of this life "light and momentary troubles": he wasn't being insensitive to the plight of those who suffer horribly in this life—on the contrary, he was one of them—but he saw that those sufferings were simply overwhelmed by the ocean of divine eternity and the joy and glory God will give to those who trust Him.

One reason the problem of evil seems so intractable to us today is because we no longer live in this perspective. To borrow Paul's phrase, we look to the things that are seen, not to the things that are unseen. As the beer commercial says, "You only go around once in life, so grab for all the gusto you can get." With such a shallow, selfish view of life, it's no wonder we can't understnd how God could permit us to suffer: it doesn't contribute to our gusto! Even as Christians, we absorb this worldly attitude. The pressures and affairs of this life seem so real and so urgent that we forget to lift up our eyes beyond the horizons of our own life to the eternal life that waits for us beyond.

But when we keep in mind that life does not end at the grave and that in heaven God "will wipe away every tear from [our] eyes; there shall be no more death, nor sorrow, nor crying; and there shall be no more pain" (Revelation 21:4, NKJV*), but only the fullness of divine joy and glory, then the problem of evil does not seem so severe. As Tolstoi once put it, "God sees the truth, but waits." In the end divine rewards and punishments will do more than enough to make up for what we have suffered here.

This account serves to highlight another element in the Christian story: knowing God is an incommensurable good. When I first became a Christian, it struck me that in order to obtain eternal life in heaven, it would be worth it if God asked us to undergo an earthly life of the most

* *New King James Version.*

extreme asceticism, suffering, and self-denial, but that God in His graciousness doesn't even ask us to do that; instead, He fills our lives with peace, joy, love, meaning, and purpose. You see, knowing the infinite God is an incommensurable good, which we do not deserve—on the contrary, according to the Christian story we deserve eternal separation from God—but which God freely bestows on us in Christ. To know God, both now and forever, is the fulfillment of human existence, what we were made for. Thus, the person who knows God in Christ, no matter what he suffers, no matter how awful his pain, can still truly say, "God is good to me," simply by virtue of the fact that he knows God, an incommensurable good.

Now we may never know why God permits any particular evil in our lives. But why should we know? Remember the York signal box mistake? Since we're not in the control tower, we shouldn't expect to be able to know why every evil is permitted by God or how it fits into His plan. But more than that: if the Christian story is true, then we don't need to know either. We are simply called upon to trust in God and His goodness no matter what the circumstances. This is not blind faith; there are good reasons to believe in God's existence, and we have the self-authenticating witness of His Spirit as well. We are not called upon to figure out why God has permitted us to suffer some evil; we are called upon to trust Him.

This is, I think, the true message of the book of Job. For many years I never really liked the book of Job because it doesn't ever explain why God permits evil in the world. God's answer to Job out of the whirlwind doesn't explain anything. But I think I've come to see the wisdom of the book of Job. God is saying, "You don't need to know why I permit terrible suffering and evil in the world. That's My business. What you need to learn is to trust Me in spite of everything." That's what Job did. "Though he slay me, yet I will hope in him" (Job 13:15a). And God rewarded him many times over. It may well be that there are evils in the world that serve no earthly good at all, that are entirely gratuitous from a human point of view, but which God permits simply that He might overwhelmingly reward in the afterlife those who undergo such evils in faith and confidence in God. To reiterate a point made earlier in another chapter, it may well be the case that God is not so much concerned with *what* you go through as with your *attitude* while you go through it.

Hence, it seems to me that there are elements in the Christian story that help to make the existence of the moral evil in the world more understandable. The purpose of human life is not happiness as such, but the knowledge of God. In order to bring us into a deeper relationship with Him, God may permit great suffering in our lives. There may be no purpose for this suffering in earthly terms at all, but it may be a summons to a greater trust in God with the prospect of a reward in heaven that is literally incomparable to the suffering, both in its greatness and duration.

But what about natural evil? Again, elements in the Christian story can help to make it more understandable. To begin with, it is important to see how inextricably intertwined natural evil is with human, moral evil. Imagine if there were no moral evil in the world, if everybody lived in accordance with the teachings of Jesus—what a wonderful world that would be! If there were a drought in Ethiopia, the world would rush to the aid of the people there to prevent famine. The wealth of the world would be largely redistributed, instead of hoarded in the materialistic Western nations. As a result, disease would greatly diminish, medical care would be more readily available, and people would live in decent housing instead of in shacks or shoddily constructed tenement houses that are demolished in natural catastrophes. Think of the mercy and the love that would be shown to those who suffer! Of course, terrible natural evils would remain and accidents would still occur, but if there were no moral evil, many natural evils would disappear or be greatly reduced.

Second, a world containing gratuitous natural evils may be necessary for people to come to a knowledge of God. God's overriding aim is for people to come to the knowledge of Himself in a free, uncoerced way. Perhaps it is just a fact that only in a world containing pointless natural suffering would people turn to God. Who knows? It may be that God has created a world containing natural evils that don't contribute to any higher good in this life but which serve as the context in which He knew people would believe and trust in Him.

Finally, the same thing may be said about natural evil that we said about moral evil. God may have simply created a world operating physically according to certain natural laws and then, for the most part, sat back and let nature run its course. Of course, He may intervene sometimes to do a miracle, but that is the exception rather than the rule. It is not wrong of Him to permit natural evils, for in the afterlife He rewards with an incommensurable good those who endure in faith those natural afflictions. Though He may not intervene physically in most cases to prevent suffering, that does not mean He is uninvolved, for by His Spirit He is ever there to strengthen and comfort the suffering.

Through these various hypotheses, which are elements of the Christian story, one raises the probability that if God exists, then the evil we find in the world would also exist. By raising this probability, one greatly reduces the force of the probabilistic problem of evil.

But let's get specific and see how this reasoning would apply to the two incidents that so graphically portrayed to me the problem of evil: the Mexican boy who slowly died from the collapse of a building and the Colombian girl who drowned in the aftermath of the mudslide. In the first place, both incidents concerned natural evils intertwined with human moral sin. The whole of Latin America has been victimized by an unjust and uncaring upper class, which has, in its lust for power and wealth, exploited the masses, leaving them poor and underprivileged. The suffering of those two children is indirectly attributable to this corrupt and un-Christian system, for if the societies in which the children lived were following Christian principles, their families would not have been forced to live in unsafe housing that was improperly located or so poorly built that it disintegrated under the stress of earthquake or rain. In a world free from sin, it's possible that neither of the tragedies would have taken place. Hence, man must shoulder some of the blame for those evils.

Why did God permit these children to suffer so? I don't know. Perhaps through the tragic death of this boy, God knew Mexican authorities would be shocked into requiring new construction standards for earthquake-proof buildings, thereby saving many future lives. Maybe He let it happen because the authorities should be so shocked. Maybe He permitted it so that some other person, facing death or illness in a hospital and seeing the reports on television, would be inspired by the boy's courage to face his own challenge with faith and bravery. Maybe God permitted the Colombian girl to slowly drown because He knew that only then would her family—or somebody else—turn to Him in faith and repentance. Or perhaps He knew that only through such a terrible incident would her family move away to a place where they in turn might come to be influenced or to influence someone else for Christ. We just don't know.

But maybe there wasn't any earthly reason why God permitted those catastrophes. Maybe they served no earthly good whatever. Perhaps the catastrophes were simply the unfortunate by-product of natural geological and meteorological laws and the children their unlucky victims. But God permitted this suffering in the lives of these children in order that they and their families might be driven into deeper dependence on Him. We don't know why God permitted this suffering, but this I do know: when that little girl and boy finally left this life and stepped into the next, Jesus enfolded them in His loving arms, wiped away their tears, and filled them with a glorious happiness beyond all expression, saying, "Well done, my child; enter into the joy of your Master." In that eternity of bliss, they will know a weight of glory beyond all comparison with what He asked them to suffer here. Therefore, the abused child of Ivan Karamazov, who beat her breast with her little fist and cried out to "dear, kind God," did exactly the right thing, bless her soul, and shall not lose her reward, whereas Ivan in his rebellion against God found life too bitter to live.

So it seems to me that the probabilistic problem of evil is far from unanswerable. To review what we've said, we first saw that even if the objection is unanswerable, that does not make God's existence improbable, for balancing off the negative evidence from evil is the positive evidence for God's existence, as well as the testimony of the Holy Spirit. We then saw that the notion of probability is itself vague and tends to vary from person to person. In particular, it is extremely difficult to establish from any evil in the world that God's existence is improbable, for God could have a morally sufficient reason for permitting that evil. We just don't find ourselves in a good position to judge. Finally, we saw that we can render the coexistence of God and evil more probable by adopting certain hypotheses from the Christian world view, for example, that God's chief end for man is knowledge of God, that there is an eternal life of divine rewards and punishments after this life, and that the knowledge of God is an unmerited, incommensurable good. Taken together, these considerations make it not improbable that God and the evil in the world should both exist.

But there is one last point which I should like to make that seems to me to constitute a decisive refutation of the problem of evil, namely, the argument that evil proves that God exists. Yes, I believe that there is actually a proof from evil for the existence of God. This remarkable fact became clear to me as I was speaking on various university campuses in North America on "The Absurdity of Life Without God." In this lecture, I attempt to show that if God does not exist, then life is without ultimate meaning, value, or purpose. For apart from God, there is no standard of value; moral values simply become either expressions of personal taste or societal conventions adopted and instilled for the purpose of living together. My conclusion was a purely negative one: I never tried to show that objective values do exist, but only that without God they cannot exist.

But I found people repeatedly objecting that we can and do recognize that objective values do exist (for example, that apartheid or child abuse is really wrong and that love of one's neighbor is really good) and that we can know these values exist whether or not we know that God exists. Now clearly, the objections the students raised didn't refute anything I had said. In fact, the Bible teaches that natural man, who has no knowledge of God, knows instinctively the moral law of God (Romans 2:14-15).

But the experience impressed upon me that we all do sense that certain acts are really right or wrong, that objective values do exist. In essence what the students had done was add an additional premise to my argument that converted its purely negative conclusion into a positive one. For now the argument looks like this:

1. If God does not exist, then objective values do not exist.
2. Evil exists.
3. Therefore, objective values exist.
4. Therefore, God exists.

Step 1 was the point I was arguing and is agreed to by many Christians and atheists alike. Step 2 is the premise furnished by the problem of evil itself. Step 3 is the conclusion supplied by the university students, who saw that the evils in the world are objectively wrong. And step 4 is the logical conclusion of the argument: since objective values cannot exist without God and objective values do exist (as shown by the evil in the world), it follows that God exists. Therefore, evil in the world actually proves that God exists.

If this argument is correct—and I think that it is—it constitutes a decisive refutation of the problem of evil. And notice that it does so without attempting to give any explanation at all for evil—we, like Job, may be totally ignorant of that—but it nonetheless shows that the very existence of evil in the world implies God's existence.

So in summary, I think we've seen that despite first appearances the intellectual problem of evil—whether in its logical or probabilistic version—can be satisfactorily solved.

But, of course, when I say "solved" I mean "philosophically solved." All these mental machinations may be of little comfort to someone who is intensely suffering from some undeserved evil in life. I recall reading, for example, that when Joni Eareckson Tada suffered her paralyzing accident, there came a parade of people through her hospital room, each offering explanations as to why God permitted this thing to happen to her. Though they were well-intentioned, to her these people took on the appearance of Job's comforters, and their rational explanations (a few of which were actually pretty good, I think) came across as cold and uncaring. But this leads us to the second aspect of the problem I wanted to discuss: the emotional problem of evil.

You see, for many people, the problem of evil is not really an intellectual problem: it's an emotional problem. They're hurting inside and perhaps bitter against a God who would permit them or others to suffer so greatly. Never mind that there are philosophical solutions to the problem of evil—they don't care and simply reject a God who allows such suffering as we find in the world. It's interesting that in Dostoyevsky's *Brothers Karamazov*, this is what the problem of evil really comes down to. Ivan never refutes the Christian solution to the problem of evil. Instead, he just refuses to have anything to do with the Christian God. "I would rather remain with my unavenged suffering and unsatisfied indignation, even if I am wrong," he declares. His is simply an atheism of rejection.

What can we say to those who are laboring under the emotional problem of evil? In one sense, the most important thing may not be what you say at all. The most important thing is just to be there as a loving friend and sympathetic listener. But some people may need counsel, and we ourselves may need to deal with this problem when we suffer. Does the Christian faith also have something to say here?

It certainly does! For it tells us that God is not a distant Creator or impersonal ground of being, but a loving Father who shares our sufferings and hurts with us. The great contemporary philosopher Alvin Plantinga has written,

As the Christian sees things, God does not stand idly by, cooly observing the suffering of His creatures. He enters into and shares our suffering. He endures the anguish of seeing his son, the second person of the Trinity, consigned to the bitterly cruel and shameful death of the cross. Some theologians claim that God cannot suffer. I believe they are wrong. God's capacity for suffering, I believe, is proportional to his greatness; it exceeds our capacity for suffering in the same measure as his capacity for knowledge exceeds ours. Christ was prepared to endure the agonies of hell itself; and God, the Lord of the universe, was prepared to endure the suffering consequent upon his son's humiliation and death. He was prepared to accept this suffering in order to overcome sin, and death, and the evils that afflict our world, and to confer on us a life more glorious that we can imagine. So we don't know why God permits evil; we do know, however, that He was prepared to suffer on our behalf, to accept suffering of which we can form no conception.[2]

I remember hearing a story once of three men who stood in the crowd before God's throne on the Judgment Day. Each had a score to settle with God. "I was hanged for a crime I didn't commit," complained one man bitterly. "I died from a disease that dragged on for months, leaving me broken in both body and spirit," said another. "My son was killed in the prime of life when some drunk behind the wheel jumped the curb and ran him down," muttered the third. Each was angry and anxious to give God a piece of his mind. But when they reached the throne and saw their Judge with His nail-scarred hands and feet and His wounded side, a "man of sorrows and acquainted with grief," each mouth was stopped, and they dropped silently to their knees.

You see, Jesus endured a suffering beyond all comprehension: He bore the punishment for the sins of the whole world. None of us can comprehend that suffering. Though He was innocent, He voluntarily underwent the punish-

2. Alvin Plantinga, "Self-Profile," *Alvin Plantinga*, p. 36.

ment for your sins and mine. And why? Because He loves you so much. How can you reject Him who gave up everything for you?

When we comprehend His sacrifice and His love for us, this puts the problem of evil in an entirely different perspective. For now we see clearly that the true problem of evil is the problem of *our* evil. Filled with sin and morally guilty before God, the question we face is not how God can justify Himself to us, but how we can be justified before Him. If Christ has endured incomprehensible suffering for us to bring us to the saving knowledge of God, then surely we can endure the suffering that He asks us to bear in this life. Think of what He endured out of His love for you, and you will be able to more easily trust Him when you walk the path of pain yourself.

So paradoxically, even though the problem of evil is the greatest objection to the existence of God, at the end of the day God is the only solution to the problem of evil. If God does not exist, then we are lost without hope in a life filled with gratuitous and unredeemed suffering. Bertrand Russell once remarked that no one can sit by the bedside of a dying child and believe in God. But what hope had Russell to offer apart from God? The answer is: none at all, for he recognized that on his atheistic view life could only be built upon the foundation of "unyielding despair."[3] God is the final answer to the problem of evil, for He redeems us from evil and takes us into the everlasting joy of an incommensurable good, fellowship with Himself.

3. Bertrand Russell, "A Free Man's Worship," in *Mysticism and Logic* (London: Longmans Green, 1918), pp. 47-48.

6

Hell

"Salvation is found in no one else, for there is no other name under heaven given to men by which we must be saved." So proclaimed the earliest preachers of the gospel in the book of Acts (4:12). Indeed, this conviction permeates the New Testament and helped to spur the mission to the Gentiles. Paul invited his Gentile converts to recall their pre-Christian days: "Remember that at that time you were separate from Christ, excluded from citizenship in Israel and foreigners to the covenants of the promise, without hope and without God in the world" (Ephesians 2:12).

The burden of the opening chapters of Romans is to show that this desolate situation is the general condition of mankind. Though God's eternal power and deity are evident through creation (Romans 1:20) and although God offers eternal life to all who seek Him in well-doing (2:7), the tragic fact of the matter is that in general people suppress the truth in unrighteousness, ignoring the Creator (1:18-21) and flaunting the moral law (1:32). Therefore, "Jews and Gentiles alike are all under sin. As it is written: 'There is no one righteous, not even one; there is no one who understands, no one who seeks God' " (3:9-11). Sin is the great leveler, rendering all needy of God's forgiveness and salvation. Given the universality of sin, all persons stand morally guilty and condemned before God, utterly incapable of redeeming themselves through righteous acts (3:19-20). But God in His grace has provided a means of salvation from this state of condemnation: Jesus Christ, by

His expiatory death, redeems us from sin and justifies us before God (3:21-26). It is through Him and through Him alone, then, that God's forgiveness is available (5:12-21). To reject Jesus Christ is therefore to reject God's grace and forgiveness, to refuse the one means of salvation which God has provided. It is to remain under His condemnation and wrath, to forfeit eternal salvation. For someday God will judge all men, punishing "those who do not know God and do not obey the gospel of our Lord Jesus. They will be punished with everlasting destruction and shut out from the presence of the Lord and from the majesty of his power" (2 Thessalonians 1:8-9).

It wasn't just Paul who held to this exclusivistic, Christocentric view of salvation. No less than Paul, the apostle John saw no salvation outside of Christ. In his gospel, Jesus declares, "I am the way and the truth and the life. No one comes to the Father except through me" (John 14:6). John explains that men love the darkness of sin rather than light, but that God has sent His Son into the world to save the world and to give eternal life to everyone who believes in the Son. "Whoever believes in him is not condemned, but whoever does not believe stands condemned already because he has not believed in the name of God's one and only Son" (John 3:18). People are already spiritually dead; but those who believe in Christ pass from death to life (John 5:24). In his epistles, John asserts that no one who denies the Son has the Father, and he identifies such a person as the antichrist (1 John 2:22-23; 4:3; 2 John 7). In short, "He who has the Son has life; he who does not have the Son of God does not have life" (1 John 5:12). In John's Apocalypse, it is the Lamb alone in heaven and on earth and under the earth who is worthy to open the scroll and its seven seals, for it was He that by His blood ransomed men for God from every tribe and tongue and people and nation on the earth (Revelation 5:1-14). In the consummation, everyone whose name is not found written in the Lamb's book is cast into the everlasting fire reserved for the devil and his cohorts (Revelation 20:15).

One could make the same point from the other epistles in the New Testament as well. It is the conviction of the writers of the New Testament that "there is one God and one mediator between God and men, the man Christ Jesus, who gave himself as a ransom for all men" (1 Timothy 2:5-6a).

Indeed, this seems to have been the attitude of Jesus Himself. Jesus came on the scene with an unparalleled sense of divine authority, the authority to stand and speak in the place of God Himself and to call men to repentance and faith. Moreover, the object of that faith was He Himself, the absolute revelation of God: "All things have been committed to me by my Father. No one knows the Son except the Father, and no one knows the Father except the Son and those to whom the Son chooses to reveal him" (Matthew 11:27). On the Day of Judgment, a person's destiny will be determined by how he responded to Him: "I tell you, whoever acknowledges me before men, the Son of Man will also acknowledge him before the angels of God" (Luke 12:8-9). Frequent warnings concerning hell are found on Jesus' lips, and it may well be that He believed that most of mankind would be damned, whereas only a minority of mankind would be saved: "Enter through the narrow gate. For wide is the gate and broad is the road that leads to destruction, and many enter through it. But small is the gate and narrow the road that leads to life, and only a few find it" (Matthew 7:13-14). A hard teaching, no doubt; but the logic of the New Testament is simple and compelling: the universality of sin and the uniqueness of Christ's sacrifice entail that there is no salvation apart from Christ.

Although this exclusivity was scandalous in the polytheistic world of the first century, with the triumph of Christianity throughout the Roman Empire the scandal receded. Indeed, one of the classic marks of the church was its catholicity, and for men like Augustine and Aquinas the universality of the church was one of the signs that the Scriptures are divine revelation, since so great a structure could not have been generated by and founded upon a falsehood. Of course, Jews remained in Christian Europe, and later the armies of Islam had to be combated, but these exceptions were hardly sufficient to overturn the catholicity of the church or to promote religious pluralism.

But with the so-called "Expansion of Europe" during the three centuries of exploration and discovery from 1450 to 1750, the situation changed radically. It was now seen that far from being the universal religion, Christianity was confined to a small corner of the globe. This realization had a two-fold impact upon people's religious thinking. First, it tended toward the relativization of religious beliefs. Since each réligious system was historically and geographically limited, it seemed incredible that any of them should be regarded as universally true. It seemed that the only religion which could make a universal claim upon mankind would be a sort of general religion of nature. Second, it tended to make Christianity's claim to exclusivity appear unjustly narrow and cruel. If salvation was only through faith in Christ, then the majority of the human race was condemned to eternal damnation, since they had not so much as even heard of Christ. Again, only a natural religion available to all men seemed consistent with a fair and loving God.

In our own day the influx into Western nations of immigrants from former colonies, coupled with the advances in telecommunications that have served to shrink the world toward what Marshall McLuhan has called a "global village," have heightened both of those impressions. As a result, the mainline denominations have to a great extent lost their sense of missionary calling or have been forced to reinterpret it in terms of social engagement, whereas people who continue to adhere to the traditional, orthodox view are denounced for religious intolerance. This shift is perhaps best illustrated by the attitude of the Second Vatican Council toward world mission. In its Dogmatic Constitution on the Church, the Council declared that those who have not yet received the gospel are related in various ways to the people of God. Jews, in particular, remain dear to God, but the plan of salvation also includes all who acknowledge the Creator, such as Muslims. People who through no fault of their own do not know the gospel, but who strive to do God's will by conscience, can also be saved. The Council therefore declared in its Declaration on Non-Christian Religions that Catholics now pray *for* the Jews, not for the *conversion* of the Jews, and it also declared that the Church looks with esteem upon Muslims. Missionary work seems to be directed only toward those who "serve the creature rather than the Creator" or are utterly hopeless. Carefully couched in ambiguous language and often apparently internally inconsistent, the documents of Vatican II could easily be taken as a radical reinterpretation of the nature of the church and of Christian missions, according to which great numbers of non-Christians are really part of the people of God and therefore not appropriate subjects of evangelism.

The difficulty of the traditional position has compelled some persons to embrace universalism and as a consequence to deny the incarnation of Christ. Thus, John Hick explains,

For understood literally the Son of God, God the Son, God-incarnate language implies that God can be adequately known and responded to only through Jesus; and the whole religious life of mankind, beyond the stream of Judaic-Christian faith is thus by implication excluded as lying outside the sphere of salvation. This implication did little positive harm so long as Christendom was a largely autonomous civilization with only relatively marginal interaction with the rest of mankind. But with the clash between the Christian and Muslim worlds, and then on an ever broadening front with European colonization through the earth, the literal understanding of the mythological language of Christian discipleship has had a divisive effect upon the relations between that minority of human beings who live within the borders of the Christian tradition and that majority who live outside it and within other streams of religious life.

Transposed into theological terms, the problem which has come to the surface in the encounter of Christianity with the other world religions is this: If Jesus was literally God incarnate, and if it is by his death alone that men can be saved, and by their response to him alone that they can appropriate that salvation, then the only doorway to eternal

life is Christian faith. It would follow from this that the
large majority of the human race so far have not been saved.
But is it credible that the loving God and Father of all men
has decreed that only those born within one particular
thread of human history shall be saved?[1]

Now in analyzing this problem it is important that we
have clear in our minds just exactly what the problem is
supposed to be.

For example, the problem is not, so far as I can see,
merely the idea that a loving God wouldn't send people to
hell. The Scriptures testify that God desires all men to be
saved and to come to a knowledge of the truth (1 Timothy
2:4; 2 Peter 3:9). Therefore, through the work of the Holy
Spirit, God draws all men to Himself, seeking to convict
them of sin and bring them to repentance. Anybody who
makes a free and well-informed decision to reject Christ
thus seals his own fate; he is self-condemned. His damnation can't be blamed on God: on the contrary, in a sense
God doesn't send anybody to hell—people send themselves.

Nor does the problem seem to me to be the idea that a
loving God wouldn't send people to hell if they are unin-
formed or misinformed about Christ. God is fair, and according to Romans 1 and 2, God doesn't judge people who
haven't heard about Christ by the same standard as those
who have. It would be unfair to condemn someone for not
believing in Christ when they've never heard of Christ.
Rather, God judges them on the basis of the light that they
do have, as God has revealed it to all men in nature and
conscience. According to Paul, all men can know through
nature that a Creator God exists, and they can know
through their own conscience God's moral law and their
failure to live up to it. Simply on the basis of nature and
conscience, then, all men everywhere should recognize
their guilt before God and repent, seeking His mercy and
forgiveness.

1. John Hick, "Jesus and the World Religions," in The Myth of God Incarnate, ed. John Hick (London:SCM, 1977), pp. 179-80.

Unfortunately, it is the sad testimony of Scripture that people don't even live up to this standard. They ignore the Creator and worship gods of their own making, and they flout the moral law, immersing themselves in immorality. Therefore, even when judged by standards much lower than those revealed in the gospel, the mass of humanity stands condemned before God. Oh, it's conceivable that a few might recognize God and His moral law and turn to Him in repentance and faith and that God might accordingly apply to them the benefits of Christ's blood so that they might be saved, but if we take Scripture seriously, then it's evident that such persons are very few. Most people choose the road to destruction despite God's revelation in nature and conscience, and since their choice is freely made, God cannot be blamed for their damnation.

Rather the real problem seems to me to be this: if God is all-knowing, as the Bible declares Him to be, then even prior to His creation of the world, God must have known who would receive Christ and be saved and who would not. But if this is the case, then certain difficult questions arise:

1. Why didn't God give more light to people who reject the light that they have, but who would have believed if only they had received more light?

2. More fundamentally, why did God even create the world at all, if He knew that so many people would not receive Christ and be lost?

3. Even more radically, why didn't God create a world in which He knew everyone would freely receive Christ and be saved?

These are hard questions! What is the Christian to reply to such inquiries? Does Christianity make God out to be cruel and unloving?

In order to answer these three questions, let's try to understand more precisely the reasoning that lies behind them. Basically, what the objection is saying is that it is impossible for God to be all-powerful, all-knowing, and all-good and yet for some people not to receive Christ. It's saying that if God really has all those attributes, then anybody and everybody who exists must be saved.

But why is this the case? There's no explicit contradiction between saying "God is all-powerful, all-knowing, and all-good" and "Some people do not receive Christ." The objector must therefore be assuming some hidden premises. Let's try to ferret out these assumptions.

It seems to me that the objector is making two implicit assumptions: (1) that if God is all-powerful, then He can create a world in which everyone freely receives Christ, and (2) that if God is all-good, then He prefers a world in which everybody is saved over a world in which some are lost. But are those assumptions necessarily true? I don't think so.

Let's look at the first assumption, that if God is all-powerful, then He can create a world in which everyone freely receives Christ. It seems to me, on the contrary, that it's possible that there are some people who would not receive Christ no matter what world God created them in. No matter how favorable their upbringing, no matter how many times they heard the gospel, no matter if they even saw miracles, they would still refuse to bend the knee and worship Jesus Christ. So long as God gives men freedom, it seems possible that some of them would under no circumstances be saved.

Now the objector might respond at this point: "OK, that's possible. But all God would have to do is just not create any of those people. Why couldn't God create a world with only persons who would receive Christ?"

But the obvious answer to that question is: it's possible that there is no such world. It's possible that in every world which God could create, someone would freely reject Christ. Again, God could force them to believe, but then that would be a sort of divine rape. Love for God that is not freely given is not truly love. Thus, so long as men are free, there can be no guarantee that they will all freely believe in Him. So it seems to me that the first assumption upon which this objection is based is not necessarily true. It may not be within God's power to create a world in which everyone freely receives Christ.

But what about that second assumption, that if God is

all-good, then He prefers a world in which everybody is saved over a world in which some people are lost? Again, this doesn't seem to me to be necessarily true. Let's concede for the sake of argument that the first assumption is true: God can create worlds in which everyone is saved. Must God always prefer one of those worlds over a world in which some people are lost? Not necessarily; for suppose that the only worlds which God can create in which everybody receives Christ are worlds which contain only à handful of people. If God created any more people, then at least one of them would not believe and so be lost.

Now I ask you: does God's goodness compel Him to prefer one of these sparsely populated worlds over a world in which multitudes freely receive Christ and are saved, though some others freely reject Christ? I don't think so. Why should the joy and blessedness of those who would receive Christ be precluded by some other people who would freely spurn God's love and forgiveness? So long as God offers sufficient grace for salvation to all men, I don't see that He is any less good for preferring a world in which some people are lost over a world in which everybody is saved.

So neither of the crucial assumptions made by our objector is necessarily true. God's being all-powerful doesn't guarantee that He can create a world in which everybody freely receives Christ, nor does God's goodness compel Him to prefer a world in which everybody is saved over a world in which some are lost. If either one of these assumptions is not necessarily true, then the objector's whole case is invalid. Since both of these assumptions fail, his case is doubly invalid.

But we can even go one step further than this. We can actually prove that it's entirely consistent to believe that God is all-powerful, all-knowing, and all-good and that many people do not receive Christ and are lost.

To begin with, since He is good and loving, God wants as many people as possible to be saved and as few people as possible to be lost. His goal, then, is to create no more of the lost than is necessary to achieve a certain number of the saved. In other words, God wants heaven to be as full as possible and hell to be as empty as possible, and He needs to find the optimal balance between these.

But it's possible that the actual world has such a balance. It's possible that in order to create this many people who will be saved, God also had to create this many persons who would be lost. It's possible that had God created a world in which fewer people go to hell, then even less people proportionately would have gone to heaven. It's possible that in order to achieve a multitude of saints, God had to accept creating an even greater multitude of sinners.

It might be objected, however, that an all-good God would not create persons who He knew would be lost as a by-product of His creating persons who He knew would be saved. But this objection doesn't strike me as true at all. Remember, God loves everyone He creates and gives sufficient grace for salvation to all men. Indeed, some of the lost may actually receive greater grace than some of the saved. But it's of their own free will that men reject God's grace and are lost. It is God's will and desire that all men be saved and come to the knowledge of the truth.

But someone might further object, maintaining that an all-good God would not create persons who He knew will be lost but who would have been saved if He had created them under other circumstances. But how do we know that there are such persons? We've seen that it's possible that some people would not receive Christ under any circumstances. Suppose, then, that God has so providentially ordered the world that all the persons who are lost are exactly such people. In that case, anybody who actually is lost would have been lost in any world in which God created him. Thus, it's possible that God has created a world which has an optimal balance between saved and lost and that those who are lost would not have freely received Christ under any circumstances. So long as such a scenario is even possible, it proves that an all-powerful, all-knowing, and all-good God is consistent with many people's not receiving Christ and so being lost.

So now we're ready to provide possible answers to the three difficult questions that prompted our discussion:

1. *Why didn't God create a world in which He knew everyone would freely receive Christ and be saved?* Answer: It may not be within God's power to create such a world. If such a world were feasible, God would have created it. But given His will to create free creatures, God had to accept the fact that some would reject Him and be lost.

2. *Why did God create the world, if He knew that so many people would not receive Christ and be lost?* Answer: God wanted to share His love and fellowship with created persons. He knew that this meant that many would reject Him and be lost. But the happiness of those who accept Him should not be precluded by those who freely reject Him. God has providentially ordered the world to achieve an optimal balance, the saved and the lost, by maximizing the number of those who accept Him and minimizing the number of those who do not.

3. *Why didn't God give more light to people who reject the light that they have, but who would have believed if only they had received more light?* Answer: There are no such people. God in His providence has so arranged the world that those who would respond to the gospel if they heard it do hear it. Those who do not respond to God's revelation in nature and conscience and never hear the gospel would not respond to it if they did hear it. Hence, no one is lost because of a lack of information or due to historical or geographical accident. Anyone who wants—or would want—to be saved will be saved.

In conclusion, it seems to me that the existence of multitudes without Christ does not logically invalidate the Christian gospel of salvation through Christ alone. On the contrary, what we've said helps to put the proper perspective on Christian missions: it is our duty to proclaim the gospel to the whole world, trusting that God has so providentially ordered things that through us the good news will come to the persons who God knew would accept the gospel if they heard it. Our compassion toward unbelievers is properly expressed, not by pretending that they are not lost and dying without Christ, but by supporting and making every effort ourselves to share with them the life-giving message of Christ.